Employment and Labour Law Toolbox

SECOND EDITION

EMPLOYMENT AND LABOUR LAW TOOLBOX

What Ontario Employers Need to Know

SECOND EDITION

PAUL WEARING
BA (Hons), MPA, LLB
Barrister & Solicitor

Employment and Labour Law Toolbox, second edition

Published in 2019 by

Irwin Law Inc.
14 Duncan Street
Suite 206
Toronto, ON
M5H 3G8

www.irwinlaw.com

ISBN: 978-1-55221-509-8
e-book ISBN: 978-1-55221-510-4

Cataloguing in Publication data available from Library and Archives Canada

Cover images © Andresr, Dmitry Kalinovsky, Dragon Images, michaeljung, Monkey Business Images, wavebreakmedia/Shutterstock.com

Printed and bound by CPI Group (UK) Ltd, Croydon, CR0 4YY

1 2 3 4 5 23 22 21 20 19

To Violet Hadleigh Wallbank

Contents

C. FINDING MORE INFORMATION

Endnotes are provided at the end of each chapter with more detailed information identifying, for example, a specific law or court decision referred to in the text. All Canadian laws, federal and provincial, and many recent court and tribunal decisions can be found for free on The Canadian Legal Information Institute's website, www.canlii.org.

Acknowledgements

I would like to thank Eveline Berrevoets, law clerk, for her assistance in formatting and proofing early drafts of the manuscript.

I thank my wife, Sara-Jane, for her continued unconditional support and understanding of the demands of my law practice, as well as my daughter, Katie Wallbank, paralegal, for patience with her father's way of doing things.

Abbreviations

ENTITIES

HRTO	Human Rights Tribunal of Ontario
MoL	Ministry of Labour (Ontario)
OLRB	Ontario Labour Relations Board
WSIB	Workplace Safety and Insurance Board (Ontario)

STATUTES

HRC	*Human Rights Code*, RSO 1990, c H.19
LRA	*Labour Relations Act, 1995*, SO 1995, c 1, Schedule A
OHSA	*Occupational Health and Safety Act*, RSO 1990, c O.1
WSIA	*Workplace Safety and Insurance Act, 1997*, SO 1997, c 16, Schedule A

CHAPTER ONE

The Regulatory Jurisdiction

What You Should Know

Employment relationships in companies regulated by the laws of Canada are governed by federal statutes (laws). In Ontario, companies that don't fall into the federal jurisdiction are governed by Ontario workplace legislation and regulations.

A. IS YOUR COMPANY FEDERALLY OR PROVINCIALLY REGULATED?

The rights and responsibilities of employers and employees are regulated by federal laws (statutes of Canada) or provincial laws (statutes of Ontario) depending on the nature of the business. If the business can be said to be a "federal work or undertaking," it is within the legislative authority of the federal Parliament. Some businesses are statutorily defined under the *Canada Labour Code* as "federal works or undertakings."[1] These businesses are as follows:

- banks
- marine shipping, ferry, and port services
- air transportation, including airports and airlines
- railway and road transportation that involves crossing provincial or international borders
- canals, pipelines, tunnels, and bridges that cross provincial borders
- telephone, telegraph, and cable systems

Applications for judicial review can be heard by three judges of the Ontario Superior Court of Justice or a single judge sitting as the Divisional Court. Challenges to provincial or federal administrative tribunal authority in matters of employment and labour law most often arise in union certification applications, employment standards compliance, human rights complaints, and occupational health and safety prosecutions.

ENDNOTES

1 *Canada Labour Code*, RSC 1985, c L-2, s 2.

2 See Canada, Employment and Social Development Canada, "Summary of Part II of the *Canada Labour Code*," online: www.canada.ca/en/employment-social-development/services/health-safety/reports/summary.html.

3 *Employment Standards Act, 2000*, SO 2000, c 41.

4 *Labour Relations Act, 1995*, SO 1995, c 1, Schedule A.

5 *Labour Relations Act, 1995*, SO 1995, c 1, Schedule A, s 116.

6 *Dunsmuir v New Brunswick*, 2008 SCC 9 at para 144.

7 *Dunsmuir v New Brunswick*, 2008 SCC 9 at para 47.

CHAPTER TWO

Considerations in the Formation of the Non-union Employment Relationship — Contract of Service

What You Should Know

The Ontario *Human Rights Code*[1] sets rules and obligations to be observed by employers in the recruiting process before an employment relationship is established. The *Code* also sets standards for the treatment of employees once an employment relationship has been established. In addition, the *Accessibility for Ontarians With Disabilities Act, 2005*[2] creates obligations to accommodate disabled persons in the job recruitment process. During employment, employee rights and minimum standards for employer obligations in the employment relationship are set out in the *Employment Standards Act, 2000*[3] and enforced by the Ontario Ministry of Labour, Employment Standards Program.

!

No matter what level of employment you are recruiting for, use printed application forms, customized for your business, and make all offers of employment in writing!

A. RECRUITMENT

When a business decides to hire employees, it recruits for a particular job. This usually involves print or Internet ads soliciting applications and resumés. Candidates may also be attracted by word of mouth. State the requirements for the job in concise language, and avoid overstating the benefits of the job. If you attract applications from persons who have stable employment at the time of the ad, you should avoid the risks of luring them away from that employment by addressing the issue in an employment contract. Such risks include being ordered to pay a greater amount of termination compensation if you must terminate their employment early in their tenure. Failing to address "early termination" in an employment agreement increases an employer's liability for termination compensation.

If you retain "head hunters" or recruiters, be specific as to what they are allowed to disclose to prospective candidates about the scope of the job and benefits, financial and otherwise.

B. JOB APPLICATION FORM

The job application form is the root document of the potential future employment relationship. It is the foundation of the employment contract, and it must disclose accurate information about working conditions such as hours of work and days of work, especially in industries that require shift work, department transfers, or multisite job transfers. It is important to avoid misunderstandings about the employment term (temporary, indefinite, or fixed), responsibilities, working conditions, and compensation on job application forms, in hiring interviews, and in offers of employment.

!

Customized job application forms are a must.

On job application forms and in job interviews, the *Human Rights Code* prohibits discriminatory questions based on race, ancestry, place of origin, colour, ethnic origin, citizenship, creed, sex, sexual orientation, gender identity and gender expression, record of offences, age, marital status, family status, or disability.[4] A prospective employer can ask whether the applicant is legally entitled to work in Canada and whether the applicant has been convicted of a criminal offence for which a pardon has not been granted. The job candidates can also be asked whether they are eighteen years old or older. The application form should indicate that if hired any falsification of information will result in dismissal for cause.

In addition, information about working conditions unique to your business should be disclosed in boldface print on the application form *above* the space provided for the applicant's signature. By signing, the applicant should be asked to acknowledge that she has understood all information on the form and has truthfully answered all questions.

C. JOB INTERVIEW

At the job interview stage, a prospective employer may ask questions that relate to bona fide requirements of the job. For a better understanding of the scope of permissible questions at the interview stage, the Ontario Human Rights Commission publication *Human Rights at Work*[5] is an excellent source of information. Also refer to Chapter 12 in this volume. The *Accessibility for Ontarians With Disabilities Act, 2005* requires employers to inform job candidates that accommodation of a disability is available in relation to materials and processes to be used in the recruitment process.[6] Successful candidates with disabilities must be informed of the employer's policies for accommodating employees with disabilities.

In addition to education and experience, a vital consideration is how the job applicant would fit within the company culture. The success of your company depends on a clear understanding by all employees of and a commitment to the values, work ethic, and standards of performance set by management. In a recent decision of the Superior Court of Justice, evidence of a corporate culture committed to honesty, trustworthiness, and mutual respect, as well as training of the company employees in the company's vision, defeated a claim of wrongful dismissal brought by an employee who had removed company product of small value without paying for it.[7]

Always check references and carefully review the applicant's resumé. Be alert to gaps in the applicant's reported career. A gap may be an indication of an experience or event that the applicant wants to cover up. Some employers are resorting to Facebook to round out the profile of job applicants.

D. OFFERS OF EMPLOYMENT

Written, detailed offers of employment and employment contracts are crucial for all jobs, regardless of the level of the job in the organization. At a minimum, offers of employment must be dated, should have employer policies — including anti-harassment and confidentiality policies —

- performance evaluations
- eligibility for bonus or incentive pay, including basis for calculating bonus or incentive pay, and standards or goals for achieving bonus[14] or incentive pay
- commission eligibility and calculation of commission, including non-commissionable activities (house accounts)
- health care benefits eligibility, including responsibility for premium costs
- life insurance eligibility, including responsibility for premium costs
- disability insurance eligibility, including responsibility for premium costs
- car allowance eligibility, including gas, insurance, and maintenance coverage where applicable
- share options eligibility
- vacation and time for taking vacation as well as entitlement to carry over vacation time
- sick leave
- termination for cause
- termination not for cause, including formula for termination compensation (complying with minimum entitlements under the *Employment Standards Act, 2000*[15]), defined components of termination compensation, and limits on continuation of disability coverage, if any
- early termination not for cause compensation
- obligation to mitigate termination compensation during fixed-pay-in-lieu-of-notice period
- terms of notice for voluntary resignation
- non-competition covenants
- non-solicitation covenants
- confidentiality covenants
- no additional representations or promises[16]
- contract interpretation according to Ontario law[17]
- addresses for serving notices to each other
- employer computer use privacy expectations
- drug and alcohol impairment consequences
- social media use
- company policies articulated in clear unambiguous language with consequences for violation of those policies stated in specific terms

For an employer to rely on and enforce the terms of any policy or other document affecting the employment relationship, the contents of which are not included in the actual employment contract, the policy or document must be referenced in the contract and attached as an appendix or schedule to the contract. Furthermore, a prospective employee must be given an opportunity to review the referenced policy or document and acknowledge this opportunity in writing before signing the contract and before commencing his first day of work.

!

Offers of employment or employment contracts presented to the new hire after she starts work are unenforceable!

Once the contract is signed and once the employee has started work, he must be given reasonable notice of any material changes to the terms and conditions of the contract.

In these circumstances, the employee has three options:[18]

1. Accept the changes, either expressly or implicitly through apparent acquiescence, in which case the altered terms will be enforceable.
2. Reject the changes and sue for damages on the basis of constructive dismissal if the employer insists on the changes.
3. Accept termination compensation from the employer and agree to the altered terms.

G. WHEN THERE IS NO WRITTEN CONTRACT

Failure to record the terms of the relationship can prove costly to an employer if employment is ended before the employee wants it to end and if there is a difference in expectations regarding compensation for a not-for-cause termination.

If there is no written record and if the employee commences an action in the courts or files a complaint with the Ministry of Labour (MoL), the dispute will be resolved on the basis of implied terms commonly associated with employment relationships, oral agreements proven through witness testimony, and representations proven to have been made by any of the parties. In these cases the overriding factor in the outcome of the dispute is always the credibility of the testifying witnesses. Where there are conflicting versions of the details of the relationship's history, adjudicators tend to give employees the benefit of the doubt unless their credibility in the witness box can be shaken. In addition, the courts place responsibility for documenting employment relationships on employers because employers are viewed to have the upper hand when it comes to negotiating terms of employment.[19]

An employee can get a remedy either by making a complaint to the MoL or by claiming for damages in the Ontario Superior Court of Justice or the Small Claims Court. Complaints regarding an employee's rights to termination compensation or an alleged constructive dismissal can be made to the MoL seeking the enforcement of the *Employment Standards Act, 2000*[20] for payment of termination pay and severance pay if applicable and vacation pay and benefits coverage if applicable. The *Employment Standards Act, 2000* sets *minimum standards for termination compensation*. Parties cannot contract out of this law: the content of employment contracts and agreements must recognize the minimum standards of the law.

A claim for termination compensation filed under the *Employment Standards Act, 2000* is reviewed by an employment standards officer and assessed and decided on the basis of whatever documentation is provided and oral representations made at a meeting convened by the officer. The decision of the officer can be challenged before the Ontario Labour Relations Board. Note that an employee does not require a lawyer to prepare her case. The MoL assists claimants in this regard. Conversely, employers should have legal representation to ensure that their rights are adequately represented and protected.

If the dismissed employee elects to seek a remedy in the courts, instead of accepting the statutory (*Employment Standards Act, 2000*) minimum, he may do so by commencing an action in either the Superior Court of Justice or the Small Claims Court. The choice of court will depend on the amount of damages sought. There is a $25,000 cap on Small Claims Court actions and no cap on damages awarded in a Superior Court of Justice action.

Best Business Practices

- Prepare a written employment agreement that is custom drafted recognizing the needs of your unique business.
- Ensure that what matters to you and your expectations of the prospective employee's deliverables are clearly spelled out.

- Draft workplace policies and performance standards suited to your specific business. Don't rely on cookie-cutter policies. Ensure that the policies comply with Ontario's workplace laws and regulations.
- Encourage the prospective employee to get legal advice on the draft agreement — insist on it in fact. This will avoid a court striking down components of the agreement or the entire agreement if at a later date you must end the relationship.

Written employment contracts can ensure some measure of predictability of employer liability for termination compensation.

ENDNOTES

1 *Human Rights Code*, RSO 1990, c H.19.
2 *Accessibility for Ontarians With Disabilities Act, 2005*, SO 2005, c 11.
3 *Employment Standards Act, 2000*, SO 2000, c 41.
4 *Human Rights Code*, RSO 1990, c H.19, s 23(1).
5 Ontario Human Rights Commission, *Human Rights at Work*, 3d ed (Toronto: Carswell, 2008), online: www.ohrc.on.ca/en/human-rights-work-2008-third-edition.
6 *Integrated Accessibility Standards*, O Reg 191/11, s 23.
7 *Agosta v Longo Brothers Fruit Markets Inc*, 2006 CanLII 16843 (Ont SCJ).
8 Constructive dismissal is discussed in Chapter 16, Section E.
9 *Titus v William F Cooke Enterprises Inc*, 2007 ONCA 573 at para 38.
10 *Jesuit Fathers of Upper Canada v Guardian Insurance Co of Canada*, 2006 SCC 21 at para 27.
11 *Sattva Capital Corp v Creston Moly Corp*, 2014 SCC 53 at para 47.
12 A discussion of contracts for service can be found in Chapter 3, Sections A and C.
13 Rules, policies, and procedures incorporated by reference into the contract.
14 The Court of Appeal for Ontario has articulated a two-part test for determining whether a terminated employee is entitled to damages on account of lost bonus:

(i) The court must determine whether the employee has a common law right to damages for breach of contract that would include compensation for lost bonus;

A. CONTRACT FOR SERVICE — THE NON-EMPLOYMENT RELATIONSHIP

Contracts for service or consulting contracts and independent contractor relationships are distinguishable from contracts of service by the liability for services provided and the tax treatment of fees paid for the service. Courts scrutinize the relationship in an attempt to determine the degree of control that the service purchaser has over the service provider. The law refers to the service provider in these instances as "a person in business on his own account."[1]

1) Independent Contractors

The interpretation of the service relationship often occurs when the Canada Revenue Agency audits the income tax returns of a taxpayer who claims to be self-employed. Factors that the Supreme Court of Canada has observed to be relevant include[2]

- the level (degree) of control of the service purchaser over the service provider's activities,
- whether the service provider provides its own equipment,
- whether the service provider has employees of its own,
- the degree of financial risk taken by the service provider,
- the degree of responsibility for investment and management of the service by the service provider, and
- the service provider's opportunity for profit.

There is no set formula for the application of each factor to the situation. Ultimately, the question to ask is, does the service provider provide services as a person in business on her own account? The relative weight of each factor will depend on the particular facts and circumstances of the case.[3] Since the Supreme Court of Canada's observations in 2001, the Federal Court of Appeal has added further analysis for consideration:[4]

- examination of the subjective intent of each party to the contract
- determination of whether the parties' subjective intentions can in fact be objectively sustained

In instances where the service provider is ruled to be an independent contractor, the work relationship can be terminated without notice on completion of the assignment or before completion of the assignment in breach of contract but without termination compensation.

B. CONTRACT OF SERVICE — THE EMPLOYMENT RELATIONSHIP

The contract of service represents the classic master-servant relationship, which is based on the employee's agreeing to provide services in exchange for pay by the employer. The essence of a contract of service is the degree of control that the employer has over the employee, including the following:

- supply of tools or equipment to the service provider
- absolute right to terminate the services of the service provider
- absolute right to set the service provider's hours of work and days of work
- right to set the method by which the service provider performs work
- service provider's lack of his own employees

Employees who are working under a contract of service, dismissed, and not dismissed for cause are entitled to statutory minimum notice of dismissal, or reasonable notice of dismissal under the common law, or pay in lieu ranging from a statutory minimum to a court assessment of pay in lieu of reasonable notice.

!

All employees owe a duty of good faith and fidelity to their employer. This duty is an implied term in all employment relationships.

The duty of good faith means that an employee must always act in the employer's best interests, avoid conflicts of interest with the employer, protect the assets of the employer, and maintain confidential information about the employer's business.

C. DEPENDENT CONTRACTORS

This is the so-called hybrid relationship most often found to be the relationship with commissioned sales agents. If a court rules that the terms of association between a business and a commissioned sales agent are those of a dependent contractor and that the contract is silent with respect to termination compensation, the court will imply a term that the contract may be terminated only upon reasonable notice and that the employer will be liable to pay termination compensation on terminating the relationship.

A strong indicator of dependent-contractor status is the extent of the contractor's economic dependency on the principal, often demonstrated by the complete or near-complete exclusivity of the relationship between the service provider and the service purchaser. In addition to the extent of economic dependency, the answers to the following questions will be indicative of the relationship:[5]

- Is the agent subject to the control of the principal — not only as to the product sold, but also as to when, where, and how it is sold?
- Does the agent have an investment or interest in what are characterized as the "tools" relating to the service?
- Has the agent undertaken any risk in the business sense, or, alternatively, is there any expectation of profit associated with the delivery of her service as distinct from a fixed commission?
- Is the activity of the agent part of the business organization of the principal for which the agent works?

ENDNOTES

1 *Wiebe Door Services Ltd v Minister of National Revenue*, [1986] 3 FC 553 at 564 (CA).

2 *671122 Ontario Ltd v Sagaz Industries Canada Inc*, 2001 SCC 59.

3 See *671122 Ontario Ltd v Sagaz Industries Canada Inc*, 2001 SCC 59.

4 *1392644 Ontario Inc (Connor Homes) v Canada (National Revenue)*, 2013 FCA 85.

5 See *Belton v Liberty Insurance Co of Canada*, 2004 CanLII 6668 at para 11 (Ont CA).

CHAPTER FOUR

Termination Compensation Considerations

What You Should Know

Employees and dependent contractors are entitled to minimum statutory termination compensation as of right without negotiation if the employment relationship is ended by the employer without cause. Employees are entitled to seek more than the minimum statutory amounts by launching a claim for damages for wrongful dismissal in the courts if they choose to do so, provided that they have not already filed a complaint with the Ontario Ministry of Labour that was not withdrawn before an order issued.

Written employment contracts can limit an employer's liability for termination compensation to the minimum standards of the *Employment Standards Act, 2000*[1] provided that a court does not interpret the terms to be unconscionable and that the language or terms of the contract are clear enough to rebut the presumption of common law reasonable notice of dismissal.

When there is a termination of employment by involuntary resignation, dismissal for cause, or dismissal not for cause, employment standards officers or courts are often called upon to resolve disputes about claims for termination pay, severance pay, or pay in lieu of notice. At common law, termination compensation is calculated on the global compensation of the employee. In other words, it is calculated on the ordinary or base pay and the commissions, health care benefits, life insurance, car allowance, bonus, share options, and pension, if any.

No termination compensation is owed to employees for dismissal for cause.

No termination compensation is owed to employees who have worked less than three months (probationary employees) unless the contrary is stated in an employment contract. However, if the employee can prove that termination was motivated by some form of discrimination, the courts and the Ontario Human Rights Tribunal will award termination compensation to the aggrieved employee including lost income, provided the employee can prove mitigation (reasonable job search without success).

There are additional circumstances in which the *Employment Standards Act, 2000* relieves an employer from paying termination pay or severance pay; see Chapter 7, Section O.

To lessen the possibility of disputes and liability to pay for not-for-cause terminations, record a precise formula for termination compensation and exclude common law damages in the employment contract. The formula *must meet the minimum requirements* for notice of termination or termination pay and severance pay, where applicable, under the *Employment Standards Act, 2000*. In a fixed-term contract, address the possibility of early termination with a specific amount or formula to avoid becoming liable for the total contract term. For example, if an employer enters into a fixed three-year term contract and decides that the employee is not needed after six months, the employer will be liable to pay the employee the remaining thirty months of pay unless there is a clause in the contract addressing compensation for not-for-cause termination before the expiry of the three-year term.

The minimum amount of notice or termination pay in lieu of notice mandated by the *Employment Standards Act, 2000* is based strictly on the employee's number of years of service. This is to be distinguished from the factors applied by the courts to claims for damages at common law, in so-called wrongful dismissal lawsuits. At common law, the employee's length of service, age, education, position in the company, experience, and skills are assessed to come up with what the court judges to be reasonable notice of termination. When considering the "length of service" component in determining reasonable notice, the Court of Appeal for Ontario observed the following:

> While short service is undoubtedly a factor tending to reduce the appropriate length of notice, reference to case law in a search for length of service comparables must be done with great care. The risk is that while lengths of service can readily be compared with mathematical precision that is not so easily done with other relevant factors that go into the determination of notice in each case . . . . The risk is that length of service will take on a disproportionate weight.[2]

In the case cited, the court increased the notice period awarded at trial to a professional employee terminated without cause after 2.53 years of service from five months to nine months.

If a person's employment is terminated not for cause, the employer may choose to give working notice, termination pay in lieu of notice, or a combination of both. Courts will rule working notice unenforceable if the employee can prove the existence of a poisoned work environment or embarrassment in the circumstances of fulfilling the working notice. And while an employer may elect to give working notice of termination, an actual payment of severance pay, where applicable, is mandatory under the *Employment Standards Act, 2000*.

Statutory severance pay under the *Employment Standards Act, 2000* is additional to termination pay and is based on the employee's length of service, the amount of the employer's payroll, and under certain defined circumstances the total number of employees being dismissed. The threshold for payment of severance pay is employee service of five years or more and an employer's payroll of $2.5 million or more a year. In Ontario, if these conditions are met, an employee who is terminated not for cause is entitled to one week of pay for every year of service to a maximum of twenty-six weeks. Special rules apply to mass terminations, as in the case of plant closures. When a permanent discontinuance of all or part of an employer's business occurs and when fifty or more employees are terminated within a six-month period, severance pay will be applicable regardless of the amount of the business's annual payroll.

Altering significant terms or conditions of an employment agreement without the agreement of the employee or without providing consideration (benefit) to the employee is unenforceable and will give rise to a claim of constructive dismissal.[3]

ENDNOTES

1 *Employment Standards Act, 2000*, SO 2000, c 41.

2 *Love v Acuity Investment Management Inc*, 2011 ONCA 130 at para 19.

3 Constructive dismissal is explained in detail in Chapter 16, Section E.

CHAPTER FIVE

Fiduciary Employees

What You Should Know

All employees owe their employer a general duty of good faith, loyalty, and fidelity, even if they are not fiduciaries. Fiduciary employees are held to a higher duty of fidelity than ordinary employees.

A job title alone does not determine fiduciary status. There must be real, substantive authority and control exercised by an employee over an employer's business to deem the employee a fiduciary employee. High-echelon managers and directors of an organization are normally found to be fiduciary employees and, as such, to owe their employer a fiduciary obligation that transcends their implied duty of fidelity as regular employees. A fiduciary duty is based on trust, loyalty, and confidence.[1] The features that the courts use to determine whether a fiduciary relationship exists are as follows:

1) The fiduciary has scope for the exercise of some discretion or power.
2) The fiduciary can unilaterally exercise that power or discretion so as to affect the beneficiary's legal or practical interests.
3) The beneficiary is peculiarly vulnerable to or at the mercy of the fiduciary holding the discretion or power.[2]

A fiduciary duty has three components:[3]

1) Avoiding all conflict of interest.
2) Acting only in the best interests of the employer.
3) Avoidance of profiting as a result of one's position.

The Court of Appeal for Ontario observed, "Without disclosure and consent, a fiduciary cannot compete with his employer during the course of his employment. After his employment ends, the fiduciary employee generally cannot directly solicit the employer's customers for a reasonable period of time . . . ."[4] Being held to a higher level of fidelity translates to a higher level of accountability for an employee deemed to be fiduciary to his employer, which in turn makes him more vulnerable to termination for cause when his misdeeds are uncovered. However, if the employer acts wrongfully in terminating the employment of a fiduciary employee, the fiduciary obligations of that employee cease.[5]

ENDNOTES

1 See *Felker v Cunningham*, 2000 CanLII 16801 at para 14 (Ont CA).
2 *Lac Minerals Ltd v International Corona Resources Ltd*, 1989 CanLII 34 (SCC).
3 See *GasTOPS Ltd v Forsyth*, 2009 CanLII 66153 at para 86 (Ont SCJ).
4 *Veolia ES Industrial Services Inc v Brulé*, 2012 ONCA 173 at para 33.
5 See *Zesta Engineering Ltd v Cloutier*, 2010 ONSC 5810.

CHAPTER SIX

Temporary Agency Workers — Whose Employees Are They?

What You Should Know

Until amendments to the *Employment Standards Act, 2000*[1] in 2009, there was confusion and litigation over the question, whose employees are temporary agency workers? The amendments sought to clarify the identity of the true employer of temporary agency workers. The law now mandates that temporary workers assigned to a client of a temporary help agency are employees of the temporary help agency.[2] But despite the statutory declaration in the *Employment Standards Act, 2000* that temporary workers supplied by an agency are the employees of the agency and not the business that they are assigned to, the Ontario Labour Relations Board will in all likelihood consider temporary agency workers assigned to a business to be employees of an employer targeted in a union certification application for the purpose of determining the number of employees in a potential bargaining unit.

When a person and a temporary help agency agree, in writing or orally, that the agency will assign or attempt to assign the person to perform work on a temporary basis for clients or potential clients of the agency, the temporary help agency becomes the employer of the person and the person becomes an employee of the temporary help agency. The employer-employee relationship between the temporary help agency and the temporary worker continues regardless of whether the worker is on assignment working for a client of the agency or not. Employment ends

CHAPTER SEVEN

Minimum Mandatory Employer Obligations — *Employment Standards Act, 2000*

What You Should Know

This law[1] is an employee's best friend. It sets minimum standards for the regulation of basic working conditions of employees who perform work in Ontario or outside Ontario if the work performed outside Ontario is a continuation of work performed in Ontario. The *Employment Standards Act, 2000* imposes obligations on employers for record keeping and job protection for specified leaves of absence. It sets standards for hours of work and eating periods and breaks. It guarantees minimum wage, overtime pay, termination pay, severance pay, if applicable, vacation pay, public holiday pay, equal pay for equal work, and continuity of employment when businesses are sold. The law protects employees from reprisals for seeking the enforcement of the standards set by the law and provides a vehicle for employee complaints and the investigation and adjudication of those complaints. It sets business conduct standards for temporary help agencies and codifies the obligations of those agencies toward temporary workers.

The law provides employees with a cost-free vehicle to obtain remedies against their employer to enforce the standards and protections mandated by the *Employment Standards Act, 2000*. Additional workplace standards for the benefit and protection of employees are mandated by the Ontario *Occupational Health and Safety Act*, *Human Rights Code*, *Pay Equity Act*, *Workplace Safety and Insurance Act, 1997*, and *Accessibility for Ontarians With Disabilities Act, 2005*.

The *Employment Standards Act, 2000* provides a broad definition of "employer" to assist adjudicators and judges in identifying an entity responsible for providing a remedy to an employee for violation of the statute.

The definition of employer includes an owner, proprietor, manager, superintendent, overseer, receiver, or trustee of an activity, business, work, trade, occupation, profession, project, or undertaking who has control or direction of, or is directly or indirectly responsible for, the employment of a person in it, and includes a person who was an employer, and any *persons treated as one employer.*[2] Persons treated as one employer are: associated or related activities or businesses carried on by or through an employer and one or more persons.[3]

As observed earlier, the purpose of the *Employment Standards Act, 2000* is to enforce minimum standards for working conditions on employers for the benefit of their employees. Classifying a service provider as an "employee" is not always a simple exercise. In fact, classification of workers is a hotly litigated issue in labour relations and at common law due to potentially onerous liability for an "employee's" rights to termination compensation and safety. As the reader learned in Chapter 3, the law recognizes certain service providers as "dependent contractors," giving them the same benefits as "employees." The factual foundation of the litigated association determines the outcome of a claim. The *Employment Standards Act, 2000* definition of "employee" can be relied on to embellish the factual foundation.

Under the *Employment Standards Act, 2000*, the definition of "employee" includes

- a person, including an officer of a corporation, who performs work for an employer for wages,
- a person who receives training from a person who is an employer, if the skill in which the person is being trained is a skill used by the employer's employees,
- a person who supplies services to an employer for wages,
- a person who is a homeworker, and
- it includes a person who was an employee.[4]

All employment contracts, whether written or oral, must meet or exceed the minimum standards set for terms and conditions of employment by the *Employment Standards Act, 2000*. An employer and employee can agree to compensation that provides a greater benefit than the minimum standard, but they cannot contract out of the minimum standard. Certain classes of employees are not covered by the law, notably employees of federally regulated employers, persons employed by the embassy or consulate of a foreign nation, students in work-experience programs, elected trade union officials, and police officers. There are further exemptions, and reference should be made to the *Employment Standards Act, 2000* and the regulations under it for a complete list.

Since 20 May 2015, and annually thereafter, every employer is required to provide each of her employees with a copy of the most recent version of the Ontario Ministry of Labour poster *What You Should Know About the Ontario* Employment Standards Act.[5] Employers are obligated to display the poster in the workplace as well.

A. RETENTION OF EMPLOYMENT RECORDS

Employers are required to collect and maintain certain records referable to their employees for mandated periods of time:

- Employee name, address, and start date must be kept for three years after the employee ceases to be employed.
- The date of birth of employed students who are under the age of eighteen must be kept until the earlier of
  - three years after the employee's eighteenth birthday or
  - three years after the employee ceases to be employed.
- For hourly workers, the number of hours worked each day and week must be kept for three years after the relevant day or week. For salaried workers, the number of excess hours worked each day and week and not exempt from the hours of work and overtime provisions of the *Employment Standards Act, 2000* must be kept for the same period.
- Vacation pay statements must be kept for three years after the vacation time has been taken.

In addition, records of pregnancy or parental leave, family medical leave, personal emergency leave, declared emergency leave, reservist leave, family caregiver leave, critically ill child care leave, and crime-related child death or disappearance leave must be kept for three years after the day on which the leave expired. All these records must be easily available for inspection by and production to an employment standards officer, if requested. Note that some of these records will be the subjects of production requests in employment litigation.

E. BREAKS

Employees are entitled to have eleven consecutive hours free from work daily and eight hours off work between shifts unless the employee and the employer agree in writing to another program. This restriction does not apply to employees who are on call.

Employees are entitled to an eating period (meal break) of at least thirty minutes for every five hours of work. The meal break does not have to be paid. But if it is a condition of employment that the employee remain at the workplace during the meal break, he must be paid during the break. Employees are not entitled to any other time off for breaks.

F. EQUAL PAY FOR EQUAL WORK

This standard protects female employees from unequal treatment in pay for doing the same job as male employees.[8] For example, a female employee who works as a cake decorator in a bakery must be paid the same rate of pay as a male cake decorator in the same bakery unless a difference in rate of pay can be explained by operation of (1) a seniority system, (2) a merit system, or (3) a system that measures earnings by quantity or quality of production.

Equal pay for equal work is not to be confused with pay equity, which is equal pay for work of equal or comparable value. Pay equity evaluation of different gender-class jobs using a gender-neutral comparison system may reveal that a female job class is being paid less than a male job class performing work that is comparable in value. And if this is the result of the gender-neutral job evaluation exercise, members of the female job class must be paid at the same rate as their male job class comparators. Pay equity is explained more fully in Chapter 11.

G. OVERTIME PAY

All non-managerial employees except truck drivers[9] are entitled to one and one-half times their regular hourly rate of pay for every hour that they work more than forty-four hours in each week. This rule applies to all employees, including part- and full-time employees, temporary workers, casual workers, and students. Managerial and supervisory employees are entitled to overtime pay if they perform non-managerial work for more than half of their workday.

Employers and employees can agree to time off in lieu of overtime pay provided that the time off is based on a calculation of one and one-half hours of paid time off for every hour of overtime worked. Employees may agree in writing with their employer to average their working hours over periods of two or more weeks to calculate overtime pay if the employer also has the approval of the Director of Employment Standards.

H. MINIMUM WAGE

This is set by the provincial government and revised periodically. It is the lowest wage rate that an employer can pay an employee regardless of whether the employee is part-time, full-time, casual, paid by commission, flat rate, or salaried. There are five categories of minimum wage:

1. General
2. Students
3. Liquor servers
4. Hunting and fishing guides
5. Homeworkers[10]

I. PAYMENT OF WAGES

Employers must establish a regular pay period (weekly, biweekly, monthly) and a regular payday. Wage statements must be issued on or before each payday explaining all deductions from the agreed-upon wage rate. The only deductions allowed to be made from an employee's pay or vacation pay are

- statutory deductions,
- court ordered deductions (garnishee orders), and
- deductions made with written employee authorization.

J. VACATION WITH PAY

Employees are entitled to two weeks' vacation time after one year of employment[11] and vacation pay of at least 4 percent of their gross wages earned in the preceding twelve months.[12] After five years of employment, an employee is entitled to three weeks of vacation time and vacation pay of at least 6 percent of their gross wages. Employers may choose to provide more vacation time and greater vacation pay benefits, but it is not a legal requirement. Employees earn vacation time while off work due to pregnancy, parental leave, family medical leave, emergency leave, or any other approved leave of absence. If a public holiday occurs during an employee's vacation time, the employee is entitled to a substitute day off with public holiday pay. The employee can agree in writing with the employer to accept public holiday pay without taking a substitute day off work. Vacation must be taken within ten months following the completion of the vacation entitlement year.

The actual time taken off by the employee for vacation is subject to the employer's choice, not the employee's. Furthermore, it is open to an employer to set rules for vacation time carry-over. Such rules must be disclosed in writing and brought to the attention of new hires before they commence employment. If the company policy is to prohibit vacation time carry-over and if an employee fails to take her earned vacation time, vacation pay must still be paid to the employee.

K. PUBLIC HOLIDAYS (STATUTORY HOLIDAYS)

Currently[13] there are nine public holidays in Ontario:

- New Year's Day
- Family Day
- Good Friday
- Victoria Day
- Canada Day
- Labour Day
- Thanksgiving Day
- Christmas Day
- Boxing Day

To qualify for a public holiday and public holiday pay, an employee[14] must work all of the last regularly scheduled day of work before the public holiday or all of the first regularly scheduled day of work after the public holiday unless there is a reasonable cause for failing to work the last (or first) regularly scheduled day before (or after) the public holiday. Alternatively, to qualify, an employee must work the entire shift on the public holiday unless there is a reasonable cause for failing to work the entire shift. The Labour Relations Board and employment standards officers have interpreted reasonable cause to mean that "something beyond his or her control prevents the employee from working."[15]

Employees who fall within the following categories can be required to work on a public holiday without their agreement to do so if the public holiday falls on a day that the employee would normally work and if the employee is not on vacation:

- hotel, motel, and tourist resort workers
- restaurant and tavern workers
- hospital and nursing home workers
- continuous operations workers

But these employees do not lose out on this statutory benefit. At the option of the employer, they are given either their regular rate of pay for hours worked on the public holiday plus a substitute day off work with public holiday pay or public holiday pay plus premium pay[16] for each hour worked.

L. PUBLIC HOLIDAY PAY

The amount of public holiday pay is based on all the regular wages earned by the employee in the four-week period before the work week with the public holiday plus all the vacation pay payable to the employee with respect to the four weeks before the work week with the public holiday divided by twenty.

M. LAYOFF

This term is greatly misunderstood. A layoff implies recall to work, not termination of employment.

A temporary layoff only becomes permanent with liability for termination pay after thirteen weeks have passed in a twenty-consecutive-week period without a recall notice to the employee. But if the employer maintains a temporarily laid-off employee's benefits for up to thirty-five weeks in any period of fifty-two weeks, the layoff only becomes permanent with liability for termination pay after the thirty-fourth week.[17]

before commencing the parental leave. Parental leave rights are available to same-sex couples. Returning employees from pregnancy or parental leave are absolutely entitled to be reinstated to their former job or a comparable job if their former job has been eliminated.

A birth mother, also defined as a "parent," is entitled to seventeen weeks' pregnancy leave. The employee must give the employer at least two weeks' written notice before commencing the leave. In addition to pregnancy leave, a birth mother is entitled to sixty-one weeks' parental leave if she takes the available seventeen weeks' of pregnancy leave. Parental leave commences as soon as pregnancy leave ends. However, the employee may choose to return to work at the end of her pregnancy leave and start her parental leave at some later date so long as she starts her parental leave anytime within seventy-eight weeks of the child's birth or the date the child first came home from the hospital. If a birth mother does not take pregnancy leave, she may take up to sixty-three weeks' parental leave.

An employer cannot force a pregnant employee to take pregnancy leave or the commencement date of the pregnancy leave. Pregnancy leave can begin no earlier than seventeen weeks before the employee's due date. However, a pregnant employee may be advised to cease working earlier due to unforeseen health problems, in which case a pregnant employee can request a medical leave of absence.

The Ontario *Human Rights Code*'s[21] "duty of accommodation" protects a pregnant employee from being dismissed if she becomes ill before the official start of her pregnancy leave.

In addition to the birth mother's parental leave, sixty-three weeks of parental leave is available to persons who are (i) adoptive parents (whether or not the adoption has been legally finalized), or (ii) a person who is in a relationship of some permanence with a parent of the child and who plans on treating the child as their own. This includes same-sex couples. Parental leave of persons for this category must start no later than seventy-eight weeks after the date the child is born or the date the child first came into their care, custody, and control.

Qualified parents are entitled to take up to thirty-five or thirty-seven weeks[22] of parental leave. A birth mother may elect to commence parental leave immediately after her pregnancy leave ends or at any time within fifty-two weeks of the birth of her baby or the date the baby first came home from the hospital.[23] Any other qualified parent must commence parental leave no later than fifty-two weeks after the birth of the baby or the date the baby came into his care, custody, and control.[24]

During pregnancy or parental leave, an employee's record of service continues unbroken. This protection is particularly important for the purpose of calculating length of service for quantifying termination or severance pay. All benefits[25] must be continued, subject to employee contributions where relevant.

2) Family Medical Leave (Job Protection for up to Twenty-Eight Weeks in Any Fifty-Two-Week Period)

The purpose of this leave of absence is to enable an employee to provide support to a family member[26] or someone who considers the employee like family who has a significant risk of death within a period of twenty-six weeks as confirmed by a qualified health practitioner.[27] "Support" is broadly defined as providing or managing psychological or emotional care. The person receiving support does not have to reside in Ontario, and the employee must put her request in writing. The twenty-eight weeks do not have to be taken consecutively. The leave is unpaid, but the employee is entitled to a record of employment so that she can apply for up to six weeks of Employment Insurance.

3) Sick Leave (Job Protection for Three Days per Calendar Year)

This leave, without pay, is available to an employee who has been employed for at least two consecutive weeks for reasons of personal illness, injury, or medical emergency. The employee is required to advise the employer of the sick leave before starting the leave or, if it is not practical, as soon as possible after beginning the sick leave. Leave is calculated in entire days; if the employee takes only a part of a day for this leave, his absence is counted as a whole day. In circumstances, employers may request reasonable evidence that the sick leave taken meets the conditions of the law.

4) Organ Donor Leave (Job Protection for up to Thirteen Weeks)

This leave is available to employees who provide a certificate from a qualified medical practitioner confirming organ donation surgery and who have worked for the employer for at least thirteen weeks. Advance written notice to the employer of at least two weeks before beginning the leave is required. Eligible organs are kidney, liver, lung, pancreas, and small bowel.

5) Reservist Leave (Unlimited Job Protection)

An employee who has been employed for at least six months and who is a Canadian military reservist is entitled to unpaid leave with unlimited job protection if deployed to an international operation or an operation within Canada to serve in dealing with an emergency or its aftermath (such as search and rescue operations following an earthquake or other natural disaster). The employer is *not* required to continue an employee's benefits coverage while the employee is on this leave.

6) Family Caregiver Leave (Job Protection for up to Eight Weeks per Calendar Year)

An employee is entitled to a leave of absence without pay of up to eight weeks per calendar year to provide care or support to the following:

- the employee's spouse
- the employee's parent, step-parent, or foster parent or the parent, step-parent, or foster parent of the employee's spouse
- the employee's child, step-child, or foster child or the child, step-child, or foster child of the employee's spouse
- the employee's grandparent, step-grandparent, grandchild, or step-grandchild or the grandparent, step-grandparent, grandchild, or step-grandchild of the employee's spouse
- the spouse of a child of the employee
- the employee's brother or sister
- a relative who is dependent on the employee for care
- any individual prescribed by regulation as a family member

The employee must inform the employer in writing that he is taking this leave, but in an emergency, notice can be given after the fact. The employee must obtain a certificate from a qualified health practitioner stating that the person whom the employee is providing care or support to has a "serious medical condition." The person receiving the care or support does not have to reside in Ontario, and the qualified health practitioner does not have to be an Ontario-qualified health practitioner.

There is no minimum length of employment required to qualify for taking this leave.

7) Critical Illness Leave (Job Protection for up to Thirty-Seven Weeks for a Minor Child and up to Seventeen Weeks for an Adult)

An employee who has been employed for at least six consecutive months is entitled to a leave of absence without pay to provide care or support to:

- a critically ill minor child, step-child, foster child, or child under the employee's legal guardianship who is under eighteen years of age for up to thirty-seven weeks if a qualified health practitioner issues a certificate declaring that the minor child is a critically ill minor child who requires the care or support of one or more family members and sets out the period during which the minor child needs the care or support; or
- a critically ill adult for up to seventeen weeks according to the same qualifiers stated for a critically ill minor child, above

8) Domestic or Sexual Violence Leave

An employee who has been employed for at least thirteen consecutive weeks may take a leave of absence if the employee, or a child of the employee, experiences domestic or sexual violence or the threat of domestic or sexual violence, for the purpose of:

- seeking medical attention for the employee or the child of the employee
- to obtain victim services
- to obtain psychological or other professional counselling
- to relocate temporarily or permanently
- to seek legal or enforcement assistance

Leave may be up to ten days in each calendar year, the first five days are paid leave and the balance of the leave is unpaid. If a paid day of leave falls on a public holiday, the employee is not entitled to premium pay for that day. A part of a day of leave taken by the employee may be deemed as one full day by the employer.

Employees meeting the qualifier may also take up to fifteen weeks of domestic or sexual violence leave within a calendar year. A "week" is defined as running from Sunday to Saturday. Weeks can be taken consecutively or separately. The employee can elect to take leave in single days out of a week, but if they do so, it is considered that they have used up one week of the fifteen weeks' entitlement.

Regardless of whether the employee takes ten days or fifteen weeks, he is only entitled to be paid for five days of leave.

9) Family Responsibility Leave

An employee who has been employed for at least two consecutive weeks may take up to three days each calendar year because of an illness, injury, or medical emergency, or an urgent matter that concerns:

- the employee's spouse
- a parent, step-parent, or foster parent of the employee or the employee's spouse
- a child, step-child, or foster child of the employee or the employee's spouse
- a grandparent, step-grandparent, grandchild, or step-grandchild of the employee or the employee's spouse
- the spouse of a child of the employee
- a brother or sister of the employee
- a relative of the employee who is dependent on the employee for care or assistance

A part of a day of leave taken by the employee may be deemed as one full day by the employer. If the employee is subject to an employment contract that contains provisions for family responsibility leave, the employee is deemed to have taken the leave pursuant to the *Employment Standards Act, 2000* entitlement.

10) Bereavement Leave

An employee who has been employed for at least two consecutive weeks is entitled to a leave of absence without pay for up to two days each calendar year because of the death of:

- the employee's spouse
- a parent, step-parent, or foster parent of the employee or the employee's spouse

- a child, step-child, or foster child of the employee or the employee's spouse
- a grandparent, step-grandparent, grandchild, or step-grandchild of the employee or the employee's spouse
- the spouse of a child of the employee
- a brother or sister of the employee
- a relative of the employee who is dependent on the employee for care or assistance

A part of a day of leave taken by the employee may be deemed as one full day by the employer. If the employee is subject to an employment contract that contains provisions for bereavement leave, the employee is deemed to have taken the leave pursuant to the *Employment Standards Act, 2000* entitlement.

11) Crime-Related Child Disappearance Leave (Job Protection for up to One Hundred Four Weeks)

An employee who has been employed for at least six consecutive months is entitled to a leave of absence without pay for up to one hundred four weeks if the employee's child, step-child, or foster child disappears and if it is probable that the child disappeared as a result of a crime. In addition, if an employee's child disappears and if it is probable that the child disappeared as a result of a crime, the employee is entitled to a leave of absence without pay for up to fifty-two weeks. Leave will be refused if the employee is charged with the crime or if it is probable that the child was a party to the crime.

12) Child Death Leave (Job Protection for up to One Hundred Four Weeks)

An employee who has been employed for at least six consecutive months is entitled to a leave of absence without pay for up to one hundred four weeks if the employee's child, step-child, or foster child died. An employee is not entitled to a leave of absence if the child died as a result of a crime and the employee is charged with the crime or if it is probable that the child was a party to the crime. Leave must be taken in one single period.

13) Emergency Leave, Declared Emergencies

This leave is without pay and is available to employees who will not be performing their duties because an emergency has been declared under the *Emergency Management and Civil Protection Act* and because

- an order has been made under the *Emergency Management and Civil Protection Act*,
- an order has been made under the *Health Protection and Promotion Act*, or
- the employee is needed to provide care or assistance to the employee's spouse or to the spouse of a child of the employee or to a parent, step-parent, foster parent, child, step-child, foster child, grandparent, step-grandparent, grandchild, or step-grandchild of the employee or the employee's spouse.

This leave preserves the employment of employees who must provide care to immediate family and some extended family members during what is normally called a national disaster.

P. TERMINATION PAY UNDER THE *EMPLOYMENT STANDARDS ACT, 2000*

Termination pay mandated by the *Employment Standards Act, 2000* is a minimum standard of compensation for job loss that all employees are *unconditionally* entitled to unless they are guilty of statute-defined misconduct or circumstances. But it is not the maximum compensation that a dismissed employee can obtain. A terminated employee can elect to accept the statutory minimum termination compensation and commence a civil action in the courts for additional compensation for wrongful dismissal.[28] The outcome of the civil action will turn on whether the employee was terminated for cause or not for cause.

The exemptions to termination compensation under the *Employment Standards Act, 2000* are analogous to but not the same as the standards set by the courts for refusing to award damages (termination compensation) in a wrongful dismissal lawsuit. The Act mandates that all employees are entitled to pay in lieu of notice of dismissal unless an employee has been guilty of one of the following:

- *Wilful misconduct*: "Wilful misconduct for the purposes of the statutes requires some deliberate or intentional act on the part of an employee. It is not enough to show that the employee failed to perform the duties he was required to perform or performed them incompetently, if it is not also shown that his acts or omissions were the product of deliberation and design on his part. Thus acts which are done carelessly, thoughtlessly, heedlessly or inadvertently *are not* acts of wilful misconduct."[29]

- *Wilful disobedience*: "Disobedience is more consistent with a deliberate act of insubordination . . . . 'Disobedience' imports the concept of a deliberate defiance of the authority of the employer, and a conscious decision to challenge that authority."[30]
- *Wilful neglect of duty*: "A person cannot be said to be guilty of wilful misconduct or wilful neglect of duty unless he is conscious of doing the act which is complained of or in omitting to do the act which is said to have been done knowing he was committing a breach of his duty and also recklessly careless, whether it is a breach of duty or not."[31]

Additionally, the following categories of persons are excluded from the statutory right to notice of termination or pay in lieu:

- those who refuse reasonable alternative employment from the employer
- those on temporary layoff
- construction workers
- those who retired in accordance with the employer's established practice provided the practice does not contravene the *Human Rights Code*
- those hired for a specific term or task
- those employed to provide professional services, personal support services, or homemaking services as defined in the *Long-Term Care Act, 1994* if they can elect to work or not when asked to do so and if their employer is a community care access corporation
- those who fail to return to work within a reasonable time after being recalled from a temporary layoff
- those terminated as a result of a strike or lock-out
- those who fail to exercise "bumping rights," where those rights exist (usually in a unionized setting)
- those who are prevented from working due to an unforeseen event at the workplace

Although construction workers are not entitled to termination or severance pay under the *Employment Standards Act, 2000*, non-union construction workers have common law rights to termination compensation and may sue their employer for damages for wrongful dismissal.[32] Unionized workers are prohibited from commencing an action for damages for wrongful dismissal against their employer because all of their employment rights are covered by a collective agreement.

Q. SEVERANCE PAY

Severance pay is paid *in addition* to termination pay to employees who have been terminated without cause if they have had five or more years of employment with the employer and if at least one of the following conditions is met:

- the employer's annual payroll in Ontario is $2.5 million or more
- the employee is one of fifty or more employees to have been terminated in a six-month period due to the closure of all or part of the employer's business

Employees may enforce their rights to be paid termination pay or severance pay by filing a claim with the Ministry of Labour.

R. LIABILITY FOR UNPAID WAGES

The *Employment Standards Act, 2000* protects two years' unpaid employee wages since 20 February 2015. Claims for unpaid wages filed before 20 February 2015 are limited to six months before the claim was filed. "Wages" here include an employee's regular earnings, vacation pay, overtime pay, termination pay, severance pay, and public holiday pay.

An employer is primarily responsible for these obligations. But if the employer fails to make payment or if the employer is insolvent, the *Employment Standards Act, 2000* makes *all the directors* of the corporation liable for six months' regular earnings, overtime pay, and public holiday pay that became payable while they were directors and for twelve months' vacation pay that accrued while they were directors. *Directors are not liable for termination or severance pay.* Employees may enforce their rights against directors for this range of compensation by filing a complaint with the Ministry of Labour within two years of their being owed the money, or, alternatively, they may seek a remedy in the courts.

ENDNOTES

1 *Employment Standards Act, 2000*, SO 2000, c 41.
2 *Employment Standards Act, 2000*, SO 2000, c 41, s 1.
3 *Employment Standards Act, 2000*, SO 2000, c 41, s 4.
4 *Employment Standards Act, 2000*, SO 2000, c 41, s 1.
5 Online: www.labour.gov.on.ca/english/es/pubs/poster.php#get_poster, amended yearly. Also, all employers are required to post in the workplace the Ontario Workplace Safety and Insurance Board poster *In Case of Injury* (Form 82, online: www.wsib.on.ca/WSIBPortal/faces/WSIBArticlePage?fGUID=835502100635000270) and a copy of the *Occupational Health and Safety Act*, RSO 1990, c O.1.
6 Director of Employment Standards, Ontario, *Information for Employees: About Hours of Work and Overtime Pay* (Toronto: Government of Ontario, 1 March 2005), online: www.labour.gov.on.ca/english/es/pubs/hours/infosheet.php.
7 *Employment Standards Act, 2000*, SO 2000, c 41, s 21.2.
8 See *Employment Standards Act, 2000*, SO 2000, c 41, s 42.
9 Truck driver pay is governed by *Exemptions, Special Rules and Establishment of Minimum Wage*, O Reg 285/01, s 18.
10 Employees who are paid to work from their homes.
11 Certain employees are exempt from this requirement.
12 The calculation of gross wages does not include vacation pay.
13 Since January 2015.
14 Full time, part time, students, and contract employees qualify, regardless of how long they have worked before the public holiday.
15 Ontario Ministry of Labour, *Your Guide to the* Employment Standards Act, 2000 (Toronto: Government of Ontario, February 2015) at 48, online: www.labour.gov.on.ca/english/es/pubs/guide/.
16 Premium pay is one-and-one-half times an employee's regular rate of pay.
17 For additional circumstances that will also delay making a temporary layoff permanent, see *Employment Standards Act, 2000*, SO 2000, c 41, s 56(2). Additional scenarios triggering liability for termination pay are outlined in *Employment Standards Act, 2000*, SO 2000, c 41, s 56.
18 *Employment Standards Act, 2000*, SO 2000, c 41, s 1(1).
19 *Employment Standards Act, 2000*, SO 2000, c 41, s 51.
20 A parent includes a birth parent, an adoptive parent, and a person who is in a relationship of some permanence with a parent of the new-born child and who plans on treating the child as his own.

Insurance Board poster *In Case of Injury* and a copy of the Ontario *Occupational Health and Safety Act*[2]

- as of 15 May 2015, order employers to conduct self-audits of their records and employment practices and report the findings to an employment standards officer (the officer can order the method and format to be used by the report)

An employee who has a complaint must complete a claims form provided by the Ministry of Labour. The completed form is then used by the Ministry of Labour to draft a notice of claim, which is delivered to the employer. The claims form encourages the employee to contact her employer to attempt to settle the claim, and if the employee has not contacted her employer about the claim, she must report why she has not done so. One of the reasons identified on the form for not contacting the employer is "You are afraid to do so." The claims form is not shared with the employer. In fact, the notice of claim is typically a form letter. Very little information is shared with the employer in the notice of claim other than a general descriptive phrase identifying the employment standard alleged to have been breached and a total amount claimed to be owed. Settlement procedures are also disclosed.

The notice of claim informs the employer that an employment standards officer will be assigned to the claim and may require the production of documents and "other evidence" relevant to the investigation. The employer is directed to complete an employer information form, which collects basic contact information about the employer. Of interest is the fact that the current employer information form does *not* ask the employer for its side of the story. Given the brevity of the information disclosed about the claim in the notice of claim, it is probably better to wait until contacted by the officer before disclosing any defence that the employer has to the allegations.

Rarely are claims resolved without a fact-finding meeting convened by the employment standards officer assigned to the claim. Employers are usually informed of the meeting by a faxed letter from the officer, who sets the time and date of the meeting without consultation with the employer or the employee. The meeting will not be rescheduled unless the employee and the employer agree to do so.

At the meeting all relevant documents must be presented, and any witnesses to the matters in the dispute must attend. This is what "other evidence" relevant to the investigation cited in the notice of claim means.

It is neither acceptable nor allowed to present witness evidence by letter. If your witness does not attend the meeting, the officer will render a decision based on what was disclosed by persons in attendance and the documents presented. The meeting is not a hearing! However the employment standards officer invites the parties to tell their stories, and the officer will interrogate attendees, if necessary. The persons in attendance are not permitted to cross-examine each other.

At the conclusion of the meeting, the officer may issue a decision or reserve and contact the parties later. In almost all cases, if the officer decides that there has been a breach of the *Employment Standards Act, 2000*, the officer will give the employer an opportunity to voluntarily agree to pay whatever amount is found to be owing to the employee. Otherwise the officer will issue an order to pay, which carries with it an administration fee of 10 percent of the amount ordered. Until recently, the maximum amount that an employment standards officer could order an employer to pay in wages[3] to one employee was $10,000. But since 20 February 2015, there is no limit to the amount of an order that an officer can issue to an employer to pay wages to an employee who has filed a complaint unless the alleged unpaid wages became due before 20 February 2015.

An employment standards officer's authority to award remedies for a breach related to one of the job-protected leaves of absence or for a reprisal is unlimited and includes the power to reinstate employees to their lost employment and compensate them for all losses arising from the loss of employment. Since 20 February 2015, claims alleging non-payment of wages are statute barred if the wages became due more than two years before the complaint was filed or before the officer's inspection commenced. If an employment standards officer conducts an investigation into a complaint of one employee about non-payment of wages and in the course of the investigation discovers that other employees are also owed wages, the officer may issue an order to pay wages to all the affected employees.

To contest an order to pay, an employer must pay the amount ordered in trust to the Director of Employment Standards and file an application for review of the order with the Ontario Labour Relations Board no later than thirty calendar days after the date on which the order was issued. The Board will set a hearing date without consultation with the parties, and at the hearing, the parties will present evidence for evaluation by the Board through documents and the oral testimony of witnesses. The Board adjudicates disputes by weighing the evidence presented and interpreting the sections of the *Employment Standards Act, 2000* that are alleged to have been breached.

A. FINES

In addition to issuing orders, employment standards officers are authorized to issue monetary penalties or fines against employers who contravene the law. A first contravention of the requirement to display the Ministry of Labour poster *What You Should Know About the Ontario* Employment Standards Act or the requirement to keep records and to have those records easily available[4] will result in a fine of $250, a second contravention of one of these obligations will result in a fine of $500, and a third contravention within a three-year period will result in a fine of $1,000.

Best Business Practices

- Maintain and store complete records of payments to all employees.
- Provide written offers of employment or employment agreements that explicitly disclose all the terms of employment and expectations.
- Do not make promises during job interviews.
- Do not speak in generalities about the job at job interviews.
- Present the job offer or employment agreement to the candidate before he starts work.
- Attach company policies to and incorporate them into offers of employment and employment agreements.
- Get signatures.
- Use a probationary period to assess the employee's performance but also to assess her compatibility with the culture of the business.
- Set measurable standards of performance.
- Make timely written assessments of employees' performance.
- Warn employees in writing of dissatisfaction with performance or conduct and the consequences of failure to meet performance expectations or to correct conduct.
- Enforce policies and codes of conduct consistently and even-handedly.

- Require that vacation requests and any other time off requests be in writing with written approval confirming the date of the employee's return to work.

ENDNOTES

1 *Employment Standards Act, 2000*, SO 2000, c 41.

2 *What You Should Know About the* Ontario Employment Standards Act, online: www.labour.gov.on.ca/english/es/pubs/poster.php#get_poster, amended yearly; *In Case of Injury* (Form 82), online: www.wsib.on.ca/WSIBPortal/faces/WSIBArticlePage?fGUID=835502100635000270; *Occupational Health and Safety Act*, RSO 1990, c O.1.

3 "Wages" here being the employee's regular earnings, vacation pay, overtime pay, termination pay, severance pay, and public holiday pay.

4 See Chapter 7.

In a unionized workplace, the employer and the union negotiate a collective agreement addressing the imposition of discipline for misconduct with a grievance procedure to challenge the penalty imposed.

ENDNOTES

1 See *Agostino v Gary Bean Securities Ltd*, 2015 ONCA 49.
2 See *McKinley v BC Tel*, 2001 SCC 38.
3 See *Haldane v Shelbar Enterprises Limited*, 1999 CanLII 9248 (Ont CA).
4 See *Carscallen v FRI Corp*, 2005 CanLII 20815 (Ont SCJ).
5 See *Carscallen v FRI Corp*, 2005 CanLII 20815 (Ont SCJ); *Potter v New Brunswick Legal Aid Services Commission*, 2015 SCC 10.

CHAPTER TEN

Safety in the Workplace

What You Should Know

The safety of employees in the workplace is primarily regulated by two laws: the Ontario *Occupational Health and Safety Act*[1] and the Ontario *Workplace Safety and Insurance Act, 1997*.[2] In addition to these laws, safety in the trucking industry is monitored and enforced through regulations to the Ontario *Highway Traffic Act*.[3]

The primary defence to charges relating to a workplace injury brought against a business is what is known as the "due diligence" defence. This means that an accused business must persuade the court that it took every reasonable precaution to prevent the workplace injury.

A. *OCCUPATIONAL HEALTH AND SAFETY ACT*

> *The Occupational Health and Safety Act* **[OHSA]** *is the main legislative vehicle for maintaining and promoting workplace health and safety standards in Ontario.*
>
> — *R v Ellis-Don Ltd*, 1990 CanLII 6968 (Ont CA), Houlden JA

It is interesting to note that the law has no "purpose" clause, unlike almost all other legislation. This omission was not by accident. Without a purpose clause, courts have much wider latitude when interpreting obligations and duties under the law.

1) The Stakeholders

This law imposes general duties and prescribed duties on employers, owners, supervisors, constructors, suppliers, licensees, corporate officers, directors, and workers to enhance and protect the safety of workers. All of these terms are specifically defined in the law. Employers shoulder a particularly heavy responsibility under the law for the safety and well-being of workers, which requires employers to be proactive in providing for training and enforcement of safety precautions in the workplace.

Not surprisingly, the *OHSA* defines a worker as a person who performs work or supplies services for monetary compensation. In addition, persons *who do not receive any pay* are also workers under the *OHSA* if they are

- secondary school students who perform work or supply services under a work-experience program, or
- persons who perform work or supply services under a program approved by a college of applied arts and technology, university, or other post-secondary institution.

Under specified circumstances, "trainees" may also be deemed to be workers.[4] Furthermore the courts have interpreted the definition of worker to include independent contractors and on-site supervisory employees.

2) Charges

Charges relating to the *OHSA* are laid under the *Provincial Offences Act* by an Ontario Ministry of Labour **(MoL)** health and safety inspector, who must swear an information (lay charges) within *one year* of the alleged offence, failing which the prosecution cannot go forward. The first notice of being charged that an employer usually receives is the MoL's service of a summons to appear in court.

Because the MoL has up to a year to file charges, if an employer is to defend the charges, it is imperative that the employer do a thorough investigation of all workplace safety incidents and store all documentation for at least a year from the date of the incident. All prepared documentation should be titled "Privileged — Prepared to Instruct Counsel" so that any pretrial motions for production of an employer's investigation reports by the Crown can be defended.

The *OHSA* creates what is known as a "strict liability" offence. This means that the Crown does not have to prove intent to commit the offence —

once the facts of the violation of the law are proven, the accused will be found guilty unless he can persuade the court that *all* reasonable steps were taken to avoid violation of the law or that he reasonably believed in a mistaken set of facts that if true would render the act or omission innocent.[5] In assessing the accused's actions, the court will consider the foreseeability of the accident and evaluate the actions of the accused on a reasonableness standard.

3) Monitoring and Achieving Health and Safety

a) Joint Health and Safety Committees

At workplaces with more than five workers but fewer than twenty, one health and safety representative for the workers and one for management must be selected.

All workplaces with twenty or more workers[6] must have a Joint Health and Safety Committee consisting of at least two persons for workplaces with fewer than fifty workers and at least four persons for workplaces with fifty or more workers. Representation must be balanced between workers and management, and management may not appoint or select worker representatives to the committee, but management is responsible to ensure that worker representatives are appointed. At least one worker representative and one management representative must be certified by the Ontario Workplace Safety and Insurance Board at the employer's expense.

The Joint Health and Safety Committee has the power to identify situations that may be a source of danger or hazard to workers, recommend improvements for health and safety in the workplace, and obtain information from the employer for the purpose of health and safety. Employers are strictly obligated to co-operate with a Joint Health and Safety Committee's request for information and with its recommendations for workplace safety. The Joint Health and Safety Committee must meet at least once every three months and keep minutes of its meetings.

b) Duties of Stakeholders

i) Workers

The obligations imposed on workers[7] by the *OHSA*[8] for their own safety really amount to common sense. That said, the *OHSA* makes the employer accountable for workers' failing to use common sense. Workers must do as follows:

supervisor is an *objective* test based on the person's actual powers and responsibilities. Whether or not a person subjectively believes s/he is a supervisor is not part of the determination. Under the OHSA, having *either* charge of a workplace, *or* authority over a worker, is sufficient for a person to be a supervisor." It is interesting to note that the guidelines suggest that a person lacking the traditional hallmarks of authority over a worker (such as the power to hire, fire, approve time off, and grant leaves of absence) may still be viewed as a supervisor if that person has some of the following responsibilities:[18]

- directing and monitoring how work is performed
- determining the tasks to be performed and by whom
- managing available resources such as staff, facilities, equipment, or budget
- deciding on and arranging for equipment to be used on a job site
- deciding on the makeup of a work crew
- deciding on and scheduling hours of work
- dealing directly with worker complaints
- directing staff and other resources to address health and safety concerns

An experienced employer would identify the above as responsibilities of lead hands. Lead hands are traditionally not recognized as supervisors in labour relations, but as far as the MoL is concerned it appears that persons who function as lead hands will be held responsible as "supervisors" for meeting the requirements of the *OHSA*.

Supervisors have specific duties under the law that in some ways mirror employers' duties. Supervisors' duties include the following:[19]

- making sure that workers work in compliance with the law and regulations
- making sure that workers use employer equipment and protective clothing or devices
- informing workers of potential or actual health or safety hazards
- taking every precaution reasonable in the circumstances for the protection of workers

Supervisors can be and are charged in relation to workplace injuries for violations of the law. Failure on the part of an employer's senior management to monitor supervisors' compliance with supervisors' duties will cause the failure of the employer's "due diligence" defence to charges. In a prosecution of charges for violation of the *OHSA*, any act or neglect by a manager, agent, representative, officer, director, or supervisor of a company charged with a violation is deemed to be the act or neglect of the company.[20]

iv) Owners

Owners of workplaces that are not construction projects are accountable to ensure that a workplace and workplace construction, development, reconstruction, alteration, or additions comply with the *OHSA* and its regulations.[21] Owners include tenants, lessees, trustees, receivers, and mortgagees in possession or occupiers of lands or premises. Persons who act on behalf of owners as agents or delegates are also accountable for compliance with the *OHSA*.

v) Constructors

The *OHSA* imposes blanket duties[22] on constructors[23] to ensure that the procedures and measures mandated by the *OHSA* and regulations are carried out. In addition, constructors are made responsible for the actions of employers and workers on a project by being accountable for employer and worker compliance with the *OHSA* and regulations on the project and being required to ensure that workers' health and safety on the project is protected.

vi) Suppliers

Suppliers of workplace equipment are responsible for ensuring that the equipment is in good condition and that it is maintained in good condition.[24]

vii) Corporate Officers and Directors

Corporate officers and directors are held accountable to take reasonable care to ensure compliance with the *OHSA*, its regulations, and any orders issued by the MoL.[25]

viii) Architects and Engineers

Architects and engineers can be charged as "suppliers" for negligent advice that results in endangering a worker.[26]

4) Right to Refuse to Work

If a worker believes that she is being asked to work in unsafe conditions or is working in unsafe conditions, which includes being subjected to workplace violence or harassment, the worker[27] can refuse to work.[28] The assessment of a situation's safety is left strictly to the worker's subjective assessment.

A worker who believes that he is working in unsafe conditions must inform a supervisor or some other representative of the employer. The employer must then investigate the situation accompanied by the worker and either a member of the Joint Health and Safety Committee (if there is no such committee, a health and safety representative) or another worker who has training, knowledge, and experience and was chosen by the workers or the union to represent the workers. If the employer is unable to satisfy the worker's concerns, a MoL inspector must be contacted to undertake an investigation of the alleged unsafe working conditions. If the MoL inspector determines that the conditions complained of by the worker are not unsafe, the worker must resume work.

A worker is absolutely protected against employer reprisals[29] for reporting unsafe work, refusing to work for safety reasons, or seeking enforcement of the *OHSA*. It is prohibited to

- dismiss or threaten to dismiss a worker;
- discipline, suspend, or threaten to discipline or suspend a worker;
- impose a penalty on a worker; or
- intimidate or coerce a worker

because the worker has acted in compliance with the *OHSA*, the regulations, or an order issued under the *OHSA*, sought enforcement of the *OHSA* or regulations, or given evidence at a coroner's inquest or in an *OHSA* enforcement proceeding.

If the employer is not unionized, a complaint against an employer for violating these worker protections is adjudicated by the Ontario Labour Relations Board. The *OHSA* imposes a reverse-onus burden of proof on an employer defending a complaint, meaning that the employer must prove on the balance of probabilities that it did not violate the protections provided to the employee. If a union represents the worker, the union may file a grievance and seek arbitration if the grievance is not resolved to the worker's satisfaction, or, alternatively, the worker or union may file a complaint with the Labour Relations Board.

Independent of a worker's refusal to work due to her perception of unsafe conditions, an employer can be directed to stop work in dangerous circumstances by a certified Joint Health and Safety Committee worker representative and management representative acting together. "Dangerous circumstances" here are circumstances in which *all* of the following are true:[30]

- a provision of the *OHSA* or the regulations is being contravened
- the contravention poses a danger or hazard to a worker
- delay in controlling the danger or hazard may seriously endanger a worker

5) Reporting Accidents

The *OHSA* imposes strict responsibilities on employers and constructors to immediately report any accident, critical injury, death, or occupational illness of a worker to a MoL occupational health and safety inspector, the Joint Health and Safety Committee, and the trade union, if any. Failure to report these occurrences in accordance with the timelines mandated by the *OHSA* will result in fines. Employers should also be aware that the MoL will investigate anonymous reports of accidents, critical injuries, or deaths of workers. There are very specific requirements for the content of reports and notices of accidents on construction projects.[31]

A critical injury is defined as an injury that does one of the following:[32]

- places life in jeopardy
- produces unconsciousness
- results in a substantial loss of blood
- involves the fracture of a leg or an arm but not a finger or a toe
- involves the amputation of a leg, arm, hand, or foot but not a finger or a toe
- consists of burns to a major part of the body
- causes the loss of sight in an eye

If a worker is killed or critically injured at the workplace,[33] an employer or constructor must notify a MoL inspector, a Joint Health and Safety Committee representative, and the trade union, if any, immediately by telephone or other direct means and send a written report to an *OHSA* "Director" within forty-eight hours of the occurrence.[34] Any wreckage, article, or thing from the occurrence must be preserved.

workplace violence should be conducted annually and after an incident of workplace violence to be able to prove a due diligence defence to future incidents.

"Workplace violence" means any of the following:[38]

- the exercise of physical force by a person against a worker in a workplace that causes or could cause physical injury to the worker
- an attempt to exercise physical force against a worker in a workplace that could cause physical injury to the worker
- a statement or behaviour that it is reasonable for a worker to interpret as a threat to exercise physical force against a worker in a workplace that could cause physical injury to the worker

Procedures for implementing the policy must include the following:

- measures and procedures to control risks identified in the workplace violence assessment exercise
- reporting incidents of threats to a supervisor or some other member of management
- investigation protocols
- consequences for violation of the policy

Additionally, the employer is responsible for informing a worker of the possible risk of workplace violence from a person with a history of violent behaviour if the worker can be expected to encounter that person at work and if the risk of violence is likely to expose the worker to physical injury.[39]

A workplace harassment policy must include reporting procedures, investigation protocols, and consequences for violation of the policy. "Workplace harassment" means engaging in a course of vexatious comment or conduct against a worker in a workplace that is known or ought reasonably to be known to be unwelcome.[40]

The law provides a definition of "workplace sexual harassment" that means:

- engaging in a course of vexatious comment or conduct against a worker in a workplace because of sex, sexual orientation, gender identity, or gender expression, where the course of comment or conduct is known or ought reasonably to be known as unwelcome; or
- making a sexual solicitation or advance where the person making the solicitation or advance is in a position to confer, grant, or deny

a benefit or advancement to the worker and the person knows or ought reasonably to have known that the solicitation or advance is unwelcome.

In addition to the definition of workplace sexual harassment stated in the *Occupational Health and Safety Act*, the Supreme Court of Canada has provided a common law definition of "sexual harassment in the workplace" in the case of *Janzen v Platy Enterprises Ltd.*[41] Chief Justice Dickson had this to say in the decision:

> Without seeking to provide an exhaustive definition of the term, I am of the view that sexual harassment in the workplace may be broadly defined as unwelcome conduct of a sexual nature that detrimentally affects the work environment or leads to adverse job-related consequences for the victims of the harassment . . . an abuse of power . . . sexual harassment is a demeaning practice, one that constitutes a profound affront to the dignity of the employees forced to endure it.[42]

The law also makes employers responsible for protecting their employees from domestic violence.[43] If an employer becomes aware or ought reasonably to be aware that domestic violence likely to expose a worker to physical injury may occur in the workplace, the law requires the employer to take every reasonable precaution in the circumstances for the protection of the worker.

8) Monitoring of Workplace Safety by the Ontario Ministry of Labour

In addition to investigating incidents of workplace injury, MoL health and safety inspectors conduct spot audits or field visits to determine compliance with the law. If the inspector finds that an employer has not posted a copy of the *OHSA*, a workplace violence policy, or a workplace harassment policy, a fine of $250 can be issued to the employer.

An inspector has very broad powers and does not need a warrant to enter any workplace or question any person at the workplace. She is entitled to test any equipment, take photographs of anything in the workplace, and demand disclosure of any document or record and take it from the workplace. She can also order an employer to provide expert reports or tests of machinery or equipment at the employer's expense. During an inspection a worker representative is expected to accompany the inspector, and the employer may also designate persons to accompany the inspector.

A visit from an inspector may be prompted by an anonymous complaint to the MoL, a spot audit, or a report of an accident in the workplace filed by an employer or constructor. Following an inspection, a field visit report may be issued. This report may direct the recipient to follow up on something that the inspector observed and that, in the inspector's opinion, needs changing to be in compliance with the law. The direction to follow up will usually require the recipient to confirm compliance with the direction within a set time frame. There is no fallout from such a direction provided that the recipient complies. On the other hand, if the inspector finds a violation of the law, he may issue an order. The recipient of an order may challenge it by making application to the Ontario Labour Relations Board within thirty days of the date the order is issued.[44] Field visit reports must be posted in the workplace, and copies provided to the Joint Health and Safety Committee or a health and safety representative.

9) Fines

Conviction of an employer for violation of the *OHSA* carries a maximum fine of $500,000. Conviction of an individual (supervisor) carries a maximum penalty of a fine of $25,000, one year in jail, or both. Typically the courts take into account the severity of the violation, the record of the accused, the size of the employer in terms of number of employees, and the financial health of the employer in assessing an amount for a fine.[45]

B. *WORKPLACE SAFETY AND INSURANCE ACT, 1997*

This law provides a no-fault insurance system for workplace injuries and occupational diseases. The primary goal of the *Workplace Safety and Insurance Act, 1997* **(WSIA)**,[46] administered by the Ontario Workplace Safety and Insurance Board **(WSIB)**, is to promote health and safety in the workplace, reduce injuries to and occupational diseases[47] of workers, and facilitate the return to work of injured employees. "Worker" is defined as anyone employed part- or full-time under a contract of service or apprenticeship with an employer, including immediate family members and relatives. Sole proprietors, partners, and executive officers in the construction industry are deemed employers for the purpose of paying premiums and deemed workers for the purpose of receiving benefits.

All employers are required to post the WSIB poster *In Case of Injury*[48] in a prominent place in the workplace, and failure to do so can result in fines being levied by WSIB inspectors.

1) Workplace Insurance Benefits

Workers receive financial and rehabilitation benefits if they suffer an injury in the course of their employment. Funding for injured workers benefits comes from premiums paid by employers that are based on the size of the employer's workforce and the employer's designated industry class. The WSIB conducts spot audits of employers to verify registration and accurate payroll reporting for the purpose of calculating these premiums.

2) Compliance

Businesses in Ontario that have employees or subcontractors must register with the WSIB within ten days of hiring their first employee. Your business can be prosecuted under the *Provincial Offences Act* for failing to register. Only banks, trade unions, trust and insurance companies, private health care practitioners, private daycare businesses, barbers, travel agencies, clubs, funeral directors, and computer software developers are exempt from registration. Notwithstanding the exemption, these businesses may elect to register.

3) Reporting Injuries and Appealing Decisions

The term "injury" is not defined in the law. A worker may be entitled to benefits under the law for traumatic "mental stress" arising out of and in the course of his employment if it can be proved that the stress is an acute reaction to a sudden and unexpected traumatic event. A pre-condition to adjudicating a traumatic mental stress claim is a diagnosis in accordance with the *Diagnostic and Statistical Manual of Mental Disorders* (DSM) that may include, but is not limited to, acute stress disorder, post-traumatic stress disorder, adjustment disorder, or an anxiety or depressive disorder.[49]

A worker is not entitled to benefits for traumatic mental stress caused by decisions or actions of his employer relating to his employment, including a change to working conditions, discipline, or discharge.

limitations, the worker's length of service, and the number of workers employed by the employer on the day of the injury.

The employer of a worker who has been unable to work as a result of an injury and who on the date of the injury had been employed continuously for at least one year by the employer shall offer to re-employ the worker.[52] This obligation does not apply to employers who regularly employ fewer than twenty employees. The obligation to re-employ continues until the earliest of the following dates:

- the second anniversary of the date of the work-related injury or illness
- one year after the worker is declared fit by the WSIB to perform the essential duties of his pre-injury job or other suitable work
- the date on which the worker reaches the age of sixty-five[53]

If an employer terminates the employment of a worker who has returned to work from a work-related injury, the worker may challenge the termination by filing a complaint with the WSIB. A WSIB case manager will determine whether the employer has violated its re-employment obligation by reviewing the circumstances of the termination to see whether or not the worker's injury or claim for benefits was a factor that contributed to the decision to terminate the worker. Employers must be prepared to disclose relevant employer policies, employee performance reviews, and reasons for termination. The decision of the case manager can be appealed by complying with set time limits for doing so.

Despite the limitations on the obligation to re-employ based on the size of the employer's workforce and the length of the injured worker's service, a person who claims or receives benefits under the *WSIA* is deemed to have a disability for the purposes of the Ontario *Human Rights Code*.[54] In addition to filing a complaint with the WSIB, such a person could file an application with the Human Rights Tribunal claiming unequal treatment on the ground of disability if her employer declines to offer to re-employ her after recovering from injury.

6) Duty of Accommodation — All Employers

> *The employer shall accommodate the work or the workplace for the worker to the extent that the accommodation does not cause the employer undue hardship.*
>
> — *Workplace Safety and Insurance Act, 1997*, SO 1997, c 16, Schedule A, s 41(6)

This obligation translates to an obligation to accommodate the injured worker with alternative work if the work performed by the injured worker before the injury is unavailable or if the worker's injuries prevent him from resuming his pre-injury job.

To determine what, if any, alternative work is available for the recovering worker, an employer is entitled to request that the worker's treating physician complete a functional abilities form, which, when completed, provides the employer with a basic understanding of the worker's physical or mental limitations. This information is then used to determine what, if any, alternative work can be offered to the recovering worker.

The Supreme Court of Canada has declared that the use of the term "undue hardship" implies an employer must accept the fact that it may experience some hardship in meeting its obligation. Considerations of business inconvenience, employee morale, customer preference, and limitations resulting from language in contracts or collective agreements are excluded when assessing the efforts of an employer to meet its obligation to accommodate. The cost of accommodation is a relevant consideration, but only a cost that would alter the essential nature of the business or one so significant that it would substantially affect the business's viability will be considered. An employer must provide documented facts to support a claim that accommodation of the injured worker will cause undue hardship for the business.

7) Construction-Industry Employers' General Duty to Re-employ — Duration of Obligation

Construction-industry employers are obligated to re-employ an injured worker until the earliest of the following dates:[55]

- the second anniversary of the date of the injury
- one year after the worker is medically fit to perform the essential duties of her pre-injury employment
- the date on which the worker declines an offer to re-employ from the employer in accordance with regulations under the *WSIA*
- the date on which the worker reaches the age of sixty-five

If an employer re-employs an injured worker and terminates the employment of that worker within six months of re-employment, the employer must prove that the termination was not related to the injury.

8) Non-union Construction-Industry Employers' Duty to Re-employ — Type of Job

If the employer is still employing workers at the workplace where the worker was injured or at a comparable workplace and if the worker is medically able to perform the essential duties of his pre-injury job, the employer must offer to re-employ him in a position in his trade (1) at the workplace where he was injured if such a position is available, or if that position is occupied by another worker who was hired after the date of the injury, displacing the other worker, or (2) at a comparable workplace if such a position is available.

If the recovered worker cannot perform the essential duties of her pre-injury job but can still work in a construction job, the employer must offer her a job in her trade at the workplace where she was injured if such a position is available. And if no such position is available, then the employer must offer her a position in her trade at a comparable workplace if such a position is available. If the employer has no suitable work in construction in her trade at any workplace, the employer must offer her a job in construction at the workplace where she was injured if such a position exists, and if no such position exists, then the employer must offer her a position in construction at a comparable workplace if such a position exists.[56]

9) Union Construction-Industry Employers' Duty to Re-employ — Type of Job

If the worker can perform the essential duties of his pre-injury job, the employer must offer him a position in his trade and classification at a unionized workplace if such a position is available or if that position is occupied by another worker who was hired, transferred, or assigned after the date of the injury, displacing the other worker.

If the recovered worker cannot perform the essential duties of her pre-injury job but can still work in a construction job, the employer must offer her a job in her trade and classification at a unionized workplace if such a position is available. And if no such position is available, then the employer must offer her a position in her trade at a unionized workplace if such a position is available. If no such position is available, the employer must offer her a position in construction at any other workplace of the employer if such a position is available.[57]

10) Records

Employers must maintain a record of all circumstances surrounding an accident reported by an injured worker. The record must contain the date and time of the incident causing the worker's injury, names of witnesses, if any, the nature and location of the injury, and the date, time, and nature of first aid given.

11) First Aid Service Capability

The law imposes a graduated level of first aid treatment capability on employers according to the number of employees on shift in the workplace. Treatment capability and first aid supplies required to be on hand increase with the number of employees on shift. Regardless of the number of employees on shift, the workplace must have a designated first aid station, first aid treatment supplies, and at least one employee with St John Ambulance Standard First Aid certification responsible for the first aid station. In workplaces with 200 or more employees on any one shift, a first aid room with a registered nurse or an employee with St John Ambulance Standard First Aid certification in charge must be maintained and stocked with various medical instruments and dressings.[58]

Best Business Practices

- Make safety your number one priority.
- Train employees in safe work practices.
- Enforce safety rules consistently and even-handedly.
- Take the work of the Joint Health and Safety Committee seriously.
- Carefully maintain and store health and safety records and Joint Health and Safety Committee minutes.

ENDNOTES

1 *Occupational Health and Safety Act*, RSO 1990, c O.1.
2 *Workplace Safety and Insurance Act, 1997*, SO 1997, c 16, Schedule A.
3 *Highway Traffic Act*, RSO 1990, c H.8; *Commercial Motor Vehicle Inspections*, O Reg 199/07; *Commercial Motor Vehicle Operators' Infor-*

ument no 15-03-02.

50 WSIB Ontario Operational Policy Manual, Chronic Mental Stress, document no 15-03-14.

51 *See Workplace Safety and Insurance Act, 1997*, SO 1997, c 16, Schedule A, s 17.

52 *See Workplace Safety and Insurance Act, 1997*, SO 1997, c 16, Schedule A, s 41.

53 The law abolishing mandatory retirement at age sixty-five does not apply to the *Workplace Safety and Insurance Act, 1997*.

54 *Human Rights Code*, RSO 1990, c H.19, s 10(1).

55 See *Return to Work and Re-employment — Construction Industry*, O Reg 35/08, s 5.

56 See *Return to Work and Re-employment — Construction Industry*, O Reg 35/08, ss 16–17.

57 See *Return to Work and Re-employment — Construction Industry*, O Reg 35/08, ss 11–12.

58 See *First Aid Requirements*, RRO 1990, Reg 1101.

CHAPTER ELEVEN

High Times

What You Should Know

On June 21, 2018, the federal government enacted the *Cannabis Act*[1] (which made it legal for persons eighteen years or older to possess cannabis (marijuana) for use in a non-public place.

This legislation caused the provinces to enact their own laws regarding the sale, purchase, and use of cannabis (marijuana).

In the province of Ontario the use of marijuana in the workplace is regulated by two laws: the *Cannabis Act, 2017* and the *Smoke-Free Ontario Act, 2017*.

In Ontario, the *Cannabis Act, 2017* prohibits a person from consuming cannabis in a public place or a workplace within the meaning of the *Occupational Health and Safety Act*. A "public place" is defined as including any place to which the public has access to as of right or by invitation, whether express or implied. A "workplace" is defined in the *Occupational Health and Safety Act* as any land, premises, location, or thing at, in, or near which a worker works.

However, the primary law[2] on the prohibition of marijuana use in the workplace is the *Smoke-Free Ontario Act, 2017*. This law prohibits smoking or holding lighted cannabis in any "enclosed public place" or "enclosed workplace" as well as some other non-work spaces designated as smoke-free and vape-free.

An "enclosed public place" is defined in the *Smoke-Free Ontario Act,*

2017, as the inside of any place, building, or structure or vehicle or conveyance, or a part of any of them,

- that is covered by a roof, and
- to which the public is ordinarily invited or permitted access, either expressly or by implication, whether or not a fee is charged for entry.

An "enclosed workplace" is defined in the *Smoke-Free Ontario Act, 2017,* as the inside of any place, building or structure or vehicle or conveyance, or a part of any of them,

- that is covered by a roof,
- that employees work in or frequent during the course of their employment whether or not they are acting in the course of their employment at the time, and
- that is not primarily a private dwelling.

The law provides for certain exemptions from the prohibition of smoking or holding lighted cannabis in any enclosed workplace in residences, if that enclosed workplace in a residence is outfitted with an indoor room. This room must be an enclosed space, designated and identified as a controlled area for the use of marijuana, and properly ventilated.

Residence is defined under the law as:

- a long-term care home within the meaning of the *Long-Term Care Homes Act, 2007;*
- a residential facility that is operated as a retirement home and that provides care, in addition to accommodation, to the residents of the home;
- a supportive housing residence funded or administered through the Ministry of Health and Long-Term Care or the Ministry of Children, Community and Social Services;
- a psychiatric facility that is designated in the regulations; or
- a facility for veterans that is designated in the regulations.

In addition, a resident who wants to use the room must be able, in the opinion of the employer, to do so safely without the assistance of an employee. Use of the room is limited to residents of the residence.

Employees of the residence are entitled to refuse to enter the room.

The *Smoke-Free Ontario Act, 2017* imposes obligations on employers to:

- ensure compliance with the law

- inform employees who work in an "enclosed workplace" of the prohibitions set out in the law
- post signage in the workplace, including washrooms, giving notice of the prohibitions
- remove ashtrays or similar equipment in an "enclosed workplace"
- remove persons who violate the prohibitions from an "enclosed workplace"

Best Business Practices

- Draft and/or amend existing company policies regarding drug and alcohol use.
- Articulate consequences for violating company rules and policies regarding drug and alcohol use.
- Address an employer's duty of accommodation for medical marijuana users.
- Post signage, clearly stating that sale and use of marijuana in the workplace are prohibited.
- Expand training to meet an employer's obligations under the *Occupational Health and Safety Act* for training its employees on safe practices.
- Consider implementing and clearly communicating a drug use testing policy to ensure the safety of all employees.
- Review policies annually, post them in the workplace, require all employees to read policies and sign off on receiving copies of the policies.

ENDNOTES

1 SC 2018, c 16.

2 Section 18 of the *Smoke-Free Ontario Act, 2017, SO 2017, c 26, Schedule 3,* states that where there is a conflict between a provision of the *Smoke-Free Ontario Act, 2017* and a regulation or a municipal by-law that deals with the subject matter to which the *Smoke-Free Ontario Act, 2017* applies, provisions of the *Smoke-Free Ontario Act, 2017* that are more restrictive shall prevail.

business. Alternatively, the tribunal will undertake an analysis of all aspects of the relationship with consideration given to the existence of any written employment contracts, the duration of the relationship, and the control of the work performed. The law states that "employee" does not include a student employed for his vacation period,[2] and under certain circumstances a casual worker is not an "employee" for the purpose of pay equity.[3]

The law does not define "employer," but the Pay Equity Hearings Tribunal has established four "tests" or criteria to be applied in determining who the employer is for the purpose of pay equity:[4]

- Who has overall financial responsibility?
- Who has responsibility for compensation practices?
- What is the nature of the business, service, or enterprise?
- What is most consistent with achieving the purpose of the *Pay Equity Act*?

A. PAY EQUITY PLAN

In non-unionized businesses, subject to the law, the employer alone is responsible for preparing a pay equity plan, which must do the following:[5]

- describe the gender-neutral comparison system used to compare the female-dominated job classes with the male-dominated job classes
- set out the results of the evaluation
- identify positions and job classes in which differences in compensation are permitted by the *Pay Equity Act*[6]
- for female job classes where pay equity does not exist, set out how compensation will be adjusted to achieve pay equity
- set out the dates on which the first pay equity adjustments will be made

When completed, the pay equity plan must be posted in the workplace for ninety days, and employees have the right to inquire into or challenge the content of the plan with the employer during this period. If during a further period of thirty days no objection is filed with the Ontario Pay Equity Commission, the plan is deemed approved.

If the employer chooses to include employee committees in preparing the pay equity plan, participants will need to be trained in gender-neutral job data collection and evaluation. The law does not require the employer of non-union employees to include them in assessing pay equity, but the outcome of the exercise will have more credibility with the workforce if employees are included, which in turn will lessen employee objections to it. Furthermore, if outcomes of the plan are challenged and investigated by a review officer or adjudicated by the Pay Equity Hearings Tribunal, the inclusion and training of employees as part of the process will improve the chances of a favourable assessment. Consultants in gender-neutral job evaluation are necessary advisers in preparing a pay equity plan.

Similar jobs are grouped together into a job class according to the gender domination of the job class. The work of the job class is given a value based on job information collection. The job information must be collected using a gender-neutral system. The common way to collect job data is to use a job questionnaire, provided the questions are gender neutral. Workplaces without men cannot assess pay equity, but under certain circumstances defined in the law a public sector employer without males in the workforce will be required to evaluate the female jobs with male jobs of another public sector employer using a proxy method of comparison.

After collecting the job information, the employer must evaluate the data for the job class using a gender-neutral comparison system applying components of skill, effort, responsibility, and working conditions. If the evaluation results for the female-dominated job class score at the same level as the comparator male-dominated job class, pay equity is achieved when members of the female-dominated job class are paid the same as their male-dominated job class comparators. Pay rates cannot be reduced to achieve pay equity, and once pay equity has been achieved, it must be maintained.

The results of the job evaluation process must be posted as part of the pay equity plan for the workplace and updated when there are changes to the job rates of the job classes evaluated or when new job classes are created. In non-unionized businesses, employees have the right to challenge the results of the job evaluation process and the job rates posted in the pay equity plan. In unionized businesses, the union has the responsibility to challenge the outcome of the job evaluation process. Complaints are investigated by a pay equity review officer, who attempts to settle them. If settlement cannot be achieved, the review officer will issue an order stating an assessment of the complaint's merits. An employer, a complaining employee, or the union in a unionized workplace may request a hearing before the Pay Equity Hearings Tribunal, which adjudicates complaints after they have been investigated by a pay equity review officer.

In unionized businesses, the law places joint responsibility on the employer and the union to prepare a pay equity plan. The employer must negotiate an evaluation process for the achievement of pay equity with the union,[7] which includes negotiating the method for the collection of job information, the gender-neutral comparison system, the gender of job classes, the value of job classes, and the calculation of the job rate. As part of the process, the union may demand disclosure of information, including financial statements, from the employer that is deemed necessary to satisfy the union's responsibility to its members to properly represent their interests in the process. Disagreements over the relevance of any disclosure demanded by the union are resolved in a hearing before the Pay Equity Hearings Tribunal, and in the experience of this writer, the tribunal will usually find that the information demanded by the union is "arguably relevant" and order its production. Once the negotiated process is successfully completed, a pay equity plan is agreed upon, and the union and the employer sign off on it, it is deemed approved.

ENDNOTES

1 *Pay Equity Act*, RSO 1990, c P.7.
2 See *Pay Equity Act*, RSO 1990, c P.7, s 1(1).
3 See *Pay Equity Act*, RSO 1990, c P.7, s 8(3).
4 See *Ontario Nurses Association v Haldimand-Norfolk (Regional Municipality) (No 3)*, 1989 Can LII 1454 (Ont PEHT).
5 See *Pay Equity Act*, RSO 1990, c P.7, s 13.
6 See *Pay Equity Act*, RSO 1990, c P.7, s 8(1).
7 See *Pay Equity Act*, RSO 1990, c P.7, s 14.

CHAPTER THIRTEEN

Freedom from Discrimination

What You Should Know

An employer "has a duty to provide a discrimination-free workplace."[1]

In Ontario, the protection of equal rights and opportunity is regulated by the *Human Rights Code* **(*HRC*)**,[2] which is administered by the Ontario Human Rights Commission. The commission drafts policies to promote and protect human rights. The Human Rights Tribunal of Ontario **(HRTO)** enforces compliance with the *HRC* through interpretation and application of the policies developed by the Human Rights Commission.

This chapter will address discrimination and harassment only in employment.

A violation of the *HRC* does not require proof of an intention to discriminate. A prohibited act once proven, regardless of the reason, will be a violation. Discrimination and harassment of persons is prohibited in employment, accommodation (housing), contracts, services, and vocational associations. The *HRC* recognizes a bona fide occupational requirement for a job, which relieves an employer of liability for what would otherwise be found to be a discriminatory policy, practice, rule, or performance standard.

Complaints alleging violation of the *HRC* are adjudicated by the HRTO and must be filed within one year of the date of the alleged inci-

obligation to determine how to accommodate the disabled employee to enable him to continue to work. The Supreme Court of Canada has established a test for determining whether a *prima facie* case of disability-based employment discrimination exists in a given situation:[13]

- Is there proof of the existence of a distinction?
- Is the distinction based on a disability or a perceived disability?
- Does the distinction have the effect of nullifying the right to full and equal exercise of human rights and freedoms?

Drug and alcohol addictions are disabilities under the *HRC*.[14]

The HRTO and the Supreme Court of Canada interpret "disability" to include past and present conditions and the subjective component of perceived disability. Furthermore, the law recognizes temporary or sporadic disabilities in addition to a permanent disability.[15]

Ableism attitudes of job recruiters/interviewers violate the HRC. "Ableism" refers to attitudes in society that devalue and limit the potential of persons with disabilities.[16] In the employment context, ableist beliefs view disability as an abnormality to rationalize the exclusion of people with disabilities from employment.

b) Family Status

Family status refers to the status of being in a parent and child relationship.[17] The Supreme Court of Canada has ruled that this goes beyond a simple parent-child relationship to embrace a parent-child relationship with a particular person.[18] The definition has further evolved to include eldercare responsibilities,[19] pregnancy,[20] and relationships with a same-sex spouse[21] and between a step-parent and a child.[22]

c) Religion

The duty of accommodation in workplace settings often arises in the context of conflicts stemming from employee requests for time off for religious holidays. It is well-established law that an employer has a duty to take reasonable steps to accommodate an employee who is unable because of religious beliefs to work in accordance with her work schedule.[23] An employer must design its workplace standards in a way that recognizes differences in religion among individual employees, and accommodate those differences.

A work schedule based on public holidays under the *Employment Standards Act, 2000* that permits time off for Christmas and Good Friday but requires work on the holy days of other religions is discriminatory. Employers have been required to allow Jewish teachers to use days of paid absences provided under a collective agreement for observing Yom Kippur.[24] If options exist under the employment agreement or collective agreement to permit time off without loss of pay, paid leave for religious observances will not be ordered. The Human Rights Commission policy on accommodation of religious observances is to provide non-Western Christians with up to two days off with pay for their religious observances unless doing so would cause an employer undue hardship. No right, including freedom of religion, is absolute.[25]

B. JOB APPLICATIONS AND INTERVIEWS

While soliciting information from prospective employees through either job applications or job interviews, employers can violate the *HRC*.

Application forms must not ask questions directly or indirectly that touch upon one of the prohibited grounds of discrimination. Photographs cannot be requested before an offer of employment is made. And requests for social insurance numbers, copies of driver's licences, and information regarding marital status, citizenship, disabilities, or availability to work shifts on specific days of the week can be made only after a conditional offer of employment has been made. Advertisements stipulating "Canadian experience" as a job qualification are considered *prima facie* discrimination (discrimination on its face) by the Human Rights Commission.[26]

Questions about a job candidate's race or sexual orientation are a violation of the *HRC*, and those about a candidate's age, sex, record of offences, or marital status may be asked only if they relate to a reasonable and bona fide qualification because of the nature of the employment.[27] Questions about citizenship are allowed if Canadian citizenship is a requirement, qualification, or consideration for the employment imposed or authorized by law.[28] Finally, the *HRC* does identify special employment circumstances that may permit questions about an applicant's ancestry, place of origin, sex, age, marital status, colour, disability, creed, or religion if the organization is primarily engaged in serving the interests of persons similarly identified and gives preference in employment to persons similarly identified and if the qualification is a reasonable and bona fide qualification because of the nature of the employment.[29]

C. DIRECT DISCRIMINATION

Discriminatory acts can be direct through statements, conduct, rules, policies, practices, or job requirements. Direct discrimination occurs when an individual is treated adversely because of a personal characteristic covered by the *HRC*. The Court of Appeal for Ontario has set a three-part test for establishing discrimination of an applicant under the *HRC*:[30]

- Does the applicant belong to an *HRC*-protected group?
- Was the applicant subjected to adverse treatment?
- Was the applicant's *HRC*-protected characteristic a factor in the alleged adverse treatment?

D. CONSTRUCTIVE DISCRIMINATION

Discrimination can also occur indirectly by applying rules or standards of performance or ability or by stipulating qualifications for job applications that would otherwise be considered neutral but *in effect* create unequal treatment of persons applying for the job.[31]

In one case, the Supreme Court of Canada found that setting an aerobic standard for applicants for government of British Columbia forest firefighter jobs prevented women from successfully competing for the jobs. Setting an aerobic standard as a minimum qualification for employment as a firefighter was held to be constructive discrimination.[32]

E. BONA FIDE OCCUPATIONAL REQUIREMENT

A job requirement, rule, or performance standard that appears on its face to be discriminatory may be acceptable if the employer can prove that it is a bona fide occupational requirement for the job. This is one of the only ways that an employer in Ontario can justify a mandatory retirement age. Otherwise mandatory retirement is against the law.

To establish that a job requirement is a bona fide occupational requirement, and therefore not discriminatory, an employer must establish all of the following on the balance of probabilities:[33]

- The purpose of the requirement is rationally connected to the performance of the job.
- The requirement was adopted in good faith in the honest belief that it was necessary.

- The requirement is reasonably necessary to the accomplishment of the work-related purpose.

To show that the requirement is reasonably necessary, the employer must be able to demonstrate that it is impossible to accommodate individual employees who are unable to meet the requirement without undue hardship to the employer.[34]

F. DRUG TESTING

> *Drug abuse [is] . . . a handicap . . . an illness or disease creating a physical disability.*
>
> — *Entrop v Imperial Oil Limited,*
> 2000 CanLII 16800 at para 89 (Ont CA)

Employers owe a duty of accommodation to employees suffering from drug abuse. The policy of the Human Rights Commission is that drug and alcohol testing is *prima facie* discriminatory and can be used only in limited circumstances. The primary reason for conducting such testing should be to measure impairment, and even testing that measures impairment can be justified only if it is demonstrably connected to the performance of the job.[35]

On-the-job testing should be administered only where a link between impairment and performance of job functions is established. Random drug testing is an unjustifiable intrusion into the rights of employees. However, the Human Rights Commission does support random alcohol testing in safety-sensitive positions, especially where staff supervision is minimal or non-existent, provided that the employer meets its duty to accommodate the needs of those who test positive.[36]

The Supreme Court of Canada has weighed in on this issue and declared that testing for drugs or alcohol must be based on evidence suggesting that there is reasonable cause to test:

> In a workplace that is dangerous, employers are generally entitled to test individual employees who occupy safety sensitive positions without having to show that alternative measures have been exhausted if there is "reasonable cause" to believe that the employee is impaired while on duty, where the employee has been directly involved in a workplace accident or significant incident, or where the employee is returning to work after treatment for substance abuse.[37]

considerations are relevant to meeting the duty of accommodation to the point of undue hardship:[51]

- Does the employer have to change the terms and conditions of the job in a fundamental way?
- Despite the accommodation, will the disabled employee remain unable to work for the reasonably foreseeable future?

An employer does not have to prove that accommodating the employee's needs would be impossible.

When an employer makes a proposal that is reasonable, it is incumbent on the employee to facilitate its implementation.[52] If the accommodation process fails because the employee does not co-operate, a complaint that the employer failed to accommodate the employee will be unsuccessful.

Even if an employee has not disclosed the fact that she is suffering from a disability, if reliable information of the disability comes to the attention of the employer, the employer has a duty to approach the employee and offer the employee an opportunity to request accommodation.

J. COMPLIANCE ENFORCEMENT

Persons who believe that their rights under the *HRC* have been violated may file an application with the HRTO naming the person or business that they claim is responsible. The application must be filed within one year of the incident giving rise to the violation, and there is *no* fee, unlike the civil courts, which require the payment of a filing fee to commence a lawsuit.

The named accused (respondent) has thirty-five calendar days after receiving a copy of the application from the HRTO to file an answer (response) to the allegations in the application. Along with answering each of the allegations in the application, the respondent must provide the names of key witnesses and a list of key documents in the respondent's possession and list any relevant documents that the respondent believes are in the complainant's possession. After the respondent files the response, the HRTO will conduct mediation of the application if both the complainant and the respondent agree to participate.

If the application cannot be settled, the matter will be scheduled for a hearing before the HRTO. For a complainant to succeed, he must present evidence of a violation of the *HRC*. The standard of proof is on the balance of probabilities (that it is more likely than not that the alleged violations occurred), and to satisfy this standard, the evidence must be "sufficiently clear, convincing and cogent."[53]

Best Business Practices

- Treat employees equally, with respect and dignity.
- Draft policies respecting human rights and post them in the workplace.
- Train supervisors and forepersons in those policies.
- Implement an internal complaints resolution procedure.
- Investigate all complaints promptly and thoroughly.
- Monitor the Human Rights Commission's policies and update your policies accordingly.

ENDNOTES

1 *McGill University Health Centre (Montreal General Hospital) v Syndicat des employés de l'Hôpital général de Montréal*, 2007 SCC 4 at para 40.

2 *Human Rights Code*, RSO 1990, c H.19.

3 This time limit is not strictly enforced by the Human Rights Tribunal of Ontario due to its discretion to waive the time limit.

4 *Arunachalam v Best Buy Canada*, 2010 HRTO 1880 at para 46.

5 *Arunachalam v Best Buy Canada*, 2010 HRTO 1880 at para 52.

6 *Russell v Indeka Imports Ltd*, 2012 HRTO 926 at para 49.

7 *Andrews v Law Society of British Columbia*, 1989 CanLII 2 (SCC), McIntyre J.

8 See Social Justice Tribunals Ontario, *Social Justice Tribunals Ontario: 2012–2013 Annual Report* at 20 & 21, online: www.ontla.on.ca/library/repository/ser/318252/2012-2013.pdf.

9 Ontario Human Rights Commission, *Policy on Preventing Discrimination Because of Gender Identity and Gender Expression* (Toronto: OHRC, 31 January 2014) at 7, online: www.ohrc.on.ca/en/policy-preventing-discrimination-because-gender-identity-and-gender-expression.

10 Ontario Human Rights Commission, *Policy on Preventing Discrimination Because of Gender Identity and Gender Expression* (Toronto: OHRC, 31 January 2014) at 7, online: www.ohrc.on.ca/en/policy-

preventing-discrimination-because-gender-identity-and-gender-expression.

11 Online: *Ontario Human Rights Commission* www.ohrc.on.ca.

12 See *Human Rights Code*, RSO 1990, c H.19, s 10(1).

13 *British Columbia (Superintendent of Motor Vehicles) v British Columbia (Council of Human Rights)*, 1999 CanLII 646 (SCC).

14 See *Entrop v Imperial Oil Limited*, 2000 CanLII 16800 (Ont CA).

15 *Quebec (Commission des droits de la personne et des droits de la jeunesse) v Montréal (City); Quebec (Commission des droits de la personne et des droits de la jeunesse) v Boisbriand (City)*, [2000] 1 SCR 665; and *Hinze v Great Blue Heron Casino*, 2011 HRTO 93.

16 Ontario Human Rights Commission, *Policy on Ableism and Discrimination Based on Disability* (27 June 2016) at 5, online: www.ohrc.on.ca/en/policy-ableism-and-discrimination-based-disability.

17 See *Human Rights Code*, RSO 1990, c H.19, s 10(1).

18 *B v Ontario (Human Rights Commission)*, 2002 SCC 66.

19 See *Devaney v ZRV Holdings Limited*, 2012 HRTO 1590.

20 See *Ward v Godina* (2 October 1994), BOI 94-030 (Ont Bd Inq).

21 See *Moffatt v Kinark Child & Family Services* (1998), 35 CHRR, D/205 (Ont Bd Inq).

22 See *Metcalfe v Papa Joe's Pizza and Chicken Inc* (2007), 225 OAC 256 (Ont Div Ct).

23 See *Ontario Human Rights Commission v Simpsons-Sears*, 1985 CanLII 18 (SCC).

24 See *Commission scolaire régionale de Chambly v Bergevin*, 1994 CanLII 102 (SCC).

25 See *Syndicat Northcrest v Amselem*, 2004 SCC 47.

26 Ontario Human Rights Commission, *Policy on Removing the "Canadian Experience" Barrier* (1 February 2013) at 3, online: www.ohrc.on.ca/en/policy-removing-"canadian-experience"-barrier.

27 See *Human Rights Code*, RSO 1990, c H.19, s 24(1)(b).

28 *Human Rights Code*, RSO 1990, c H.19, s 16(1).

29 *Human Rights Code*, RSO 1990, c H.19, s 24(1)(a).

30 *Shaw v Phipps*, 2012 ONCA 155.

31 See *Human Rights Code*, RSO 1990, c H.19, s 11.

32 *British Columbia (Public Service Employee Relations Commission) v BCGSEU*, 1999 CanLII 652 (SCC).

33 *British Columbia (Public Service Employee Relations Commission) v BCGSEU*, 1999 CanLII 652 (SCC).

34 *Jeppesen v Ancaster (Town)*, 2001 CanLII 26209 (Ont HRT).

35 See Ontario Human Rights Commission, *Policy on Drug and Alcohol Testing 2016* (2016) at 4, online: www.ohrc.on.ca/en/policy-drug-and-alcohol-testing.

36 See Ontario Human Rights Commission, *Policy on Drug and Alcohol Testing 2016* (2016) at 8, online: www.ohrc.on.ca/en/policy-drug-and-alcohol-testing.

37 *Communications, Energy and Paperworkers Union of Canada, Local 30 v Irving Pulp & Paper, Ltd*, 2013 SCC 34 at para 30.

38 See *Human Rights Code*, RSO 1990, c H.19, s 5(2).

39 *Human Rights Code*, RSO 1990, c H.19, s 10(1).

40 See *Streeter v HR Technologies*, 2009 HRTO 841 at para 33.

41 *AB v Joe Singer Shoes Limited*, 2018 HRTO 107.

42 See *Human Rights Code*, RSO 1990, c H.19, s 5(1).

43 See *General Motors of Canada Limited v Johnson*, 2013 ONCA 502.

44 See *Human Rights Code*, RSO 1990, c H.19, s 17(2).

45 See *Hydro-Québec v Syndicat des employé-e-s de techniques professionnelles et de bureau d'Hydro-Québec, section locale 2000 (SCFP-FTQ)*, 2008 SCC 43.

46 See *McGill University Health Centre (Montreal General Hospital) v Syndicat des employés de l'Hôpital général de Montréal*, 2007 SCC 4.

47 *British Columbia (Public Service Employee Relations Commission) v BCGSEU*, 1999 CanLII 652 (SCC).

48 See *Commission scolaire régionale de Chambly v Bergevin*, 1994 CanLII 102 (SCC).

49 See *Human Rights Code*, RSO 1990, c H.19, s 17(2).

50 See *British Columbia (Superintendent of Motor Vehicles) v British Columbia (Council of Human Rights)*, 1999 CanLII 646 (SCC).

51 See *Hydro-Québec v Syndicat des employé-e-s de techniques professionnelles et de bureau d'Hydro-Québec, section locale 2000 (SCFP-FTQ)*, 2008 SCC 43.

52 See *McGill University Health Centre (Montreal General Hospital) v Syndicat des employés de l'Hôpital général de Montréal*, 2007 SCC 4.

53 See *FH v McDougall*, 2008 SCC 53 at para 46.

- During the recruitment process, candidates selected for interviews must be informed that accommodation of a disability will be available in relation to the materials or processes to be used.
- If a candidate requests an accommodation, the employer must consult with the candidate and provide a suitable accommodation to address the candidate's needs due to disability.
- Successful job candidates with disabilities must be informed of the employer's policies for accommodating employees with disabilities.
- All of a business's employees must be informed of the employer's policies to support employees with disabilities, including job accommodation.
- Employers are required to consult with and provide accessible formats and communication supports to employees with disabilities to enable them to do their job.
- Employers are required to provide *individualized* workplace emergency response information to employees with disabilities if a disability is such that individualized information is necessary.
- Employers with more than fifty employees must have a written process for the development of documented individual accommodation plans for employees with disabilities and a return-to-work process for employees who are absent due to a disability and require disability-related accommodation to return to work.
- In businesses where "performance management"[4] is used to measure employee productivity, assessments must take into account the accessibility needs of employees with disabilities as well as individual accommodation plans.
- "Career development and advancement"[5] programs must take into account the needs of employees with disabilities as well as individual accommodation plans.
- Reassignment of employees to other departments or jobs within an organization as an alternative to layoff when a job or department is eliminated must take into account the accessibility needs of employees with disabilities as well as individual accommodation plans.

ENDNOTES

1 *Accessibility for Ontarians With Disabilities Act, 2005*, SO 2005, c 11.

2 *Human Rights Code*, RSO 1990, c H.19.

3 *Integrated Accessibility Standards*, O Reg 191/11.

4 "Performance management" is defined in the law as activities related to assessing and improving employee performance, productivity, and effectiveness with a goal of facilitating employee success.

5 "Career development and advancement" recognizes the movement of an employee in an organization from one job to another that may provide higher pay, provide greater responsibility, or be at a higher level in the organization.

CHAPTER FIFTEEN

Privacy in the Workplace

What You Should Know

Employees have a reasonable and continuous expectation of privacy in the personal information stored on a work-issued computer, but it is a diminished expectation subject to considerations of the truth-seeking function of the criminal trial process.

A. COMPUTER PRIVACY FOR EMPLOYEES

R v Cole[1] was the criminal trial of a teacher who had stored nude and partially nude photographs of a female student on a laptop computer issued by the school board. The photographs were discovered on a routine maintenance inspection by a school board technician. The school board handed the laptop over to the police, and the teacher was charged with possession of child pornography. At first instance the teacher was acquitted on the basis of a violation of his rights under the *Canadian Charter of Rights and Freedoms*, because the police had had no warrant for the seizure of the laptop and the files on it.

The case wound its way to the Supreme Court of Canada, where the Court ruled that notwithstanding the teacher's reasonable expectation of privacy, considerations of the criminal trial process outweighed the teacher's privacy rights. It is important to note that the school board had not required teachers to sign an acceptable use of equipment agreement and had no policy on the searching of work-issued computers or

CHAPTER SIXTEEN

Foreign Worker Protection

What You Should Know

On 20 November 2015, Ontario legislation for the protection of the rights of foreign workers, the *Employment Protection for Foreign Nationals Act (Live-in Caregivers and Others), 2009,* was repealed and replaced with the *Employment Protection for Foreign Nationals Act, 2009*[1] as of 20 November 2015. The new law expands protection of foreign nationals employed in Ontario as live-in caregivers to all foreign nationals employed or attempting to find employment in Ontario pursuant to an immigration or foreign temporary employee program. The expanded law is of significance to the service industry and the construction industry. It requires employers and recruiters to provide foreign nationals belonging to listed categories with information prepared and published by the Director of Employment Standards.

The law prohibits recruiters from charging fees to foreign nationals either directly or indirectly. Furthermore the law protects the listed categories of foreign nationals from intimidation by employers or recruiters in response to asking about or asserting any rights under the law. These rules continue to apply under the amended law.

ENDNOTES

1 *Employment Protection for Foreign Nationals Act, 2009*, SO 2009, c 32.

CHAPTER SEVENTEEN

End of the Non-union Employment Relationship

What You Should Know

Leaving aside divine intervention, there are eight ways that non-union employment may end:

- resignation
- by operation of law
- expiration of a fixed-term contract
- early termination of a fixed-term contract
- dismissal for cause
- constructive dismissal
- dismissal not for cause
- frustration of the employment contract

Except for constructive dismissal, regardless of which event triggers the termination of the employment, a personal meeting with the employee supported by notice in writing is a must. Immediately after the meeting, an employer should make notes of what was said by all parties in the meeting as an *aide-mémoire*. The meeting must be conducted with respect and dignity. High-handed, abusive conduct, regardless of the reason for dismissal, can be cause for increased damages if the termination becomes litigious. So as to avoid parading the employee in front of co-workers during the regular workday, invite the employee to return to her workstation to retrieve personal items after regular work hours.

differently.[8] Seasonal employment contract employees are also denied termination compensation when the season ends provided that the true nature of their employment does not tend to look like employment of an indefinite duration.

However, if a fixed-term contract is terminated not for cause before the expiration of the term, the employee is entitled to damages equal to the unexpired term of the contract unless the contract stipulates otherwise. Including a fixed amount of termination compensation in a fixed-term employment contract provides certainty and caps the employer's liability if the contract is terminated early. For contracts of indefinite duration, termination compensation for not-for-cause dismissal should also be spelled out to cap the employer's liability for notice of termination or pay in lieu. Failure to include specific termination compensation for not-for-cause dismissal will leave the issue open to assessment under common law principles of reasonable notice. In both types of contracts, the amount of termination compensation must meet the minimum termination compensation entitlements under the *Employment Standards Act, 2000*. Also, the employee's duty to mitigate damages must be spelled out to prevent her from getting a windfall of termination compensation if she is able to become re-employed sooner than the termination compensation payments run out.

D. DISMISSAL FOR CAUSE

Dismissal for cause denies the employee any compensation. An employee's gross incompetence or dissatisfaction with an employee's performance, honesty, or illegal drug use may cause an employer to want to terminate the employment relationship for cause.

The courts apply a contextual analysis to the impugned conduct to determine whether the penalty of dismissal for cause is proportional to the misconduct. Expressed as a question, the courts ask, Does the impugned conduct irreparably harm the employment relationship? Not all misconduct warrants summary dismissal, and an effective balance must be struck between the severity of an employee's misconduct and the sanction imposed.[9] The employer bears the onus of persuading the court on the balance of probabilities that cause exists. It must prove to the court's satisfaction that there were no other reasonable alternatives to termination.[10]

The nature and circumstances of the impugned conduct must be assessed. The following factors have been considered relevant in assessing the circumstances:

- whether the employee was guilty of serious misconduct;
- whether the employee's impugned behaviour or act was merely conduct with which the employer disagreed, or "trifling causes", rather than transgressions or misconduct which any reasonable person could not overlook;
- whether the employee's misconduct was inconsistent with or prejudicial to the employer's business, and therefore in breach of an implied term of the employment agreement;
- whether the employee's misconduct was in breach of an express provision of the employment agreement; . . .
- whether the misconduct merely reflects the employee's poor judgment . . . .
- whether the employee was culpable for alleged criminal conduct, or misconduct of a criminal nature;
- whether the conduct was prejudicial or inimical to the employer's legitimate business interests;
- whether the conduct was in breach of the implied duty of fidelity, or fiduciary duty, or an express condition of employment, and therefore in breach of the employment agreement;
- whether there is evidence of actual harm or evidence substantiating potential harm to the employer.[11]

To determine whether an employer was justified in dismissing an employee for misconduct, a court will make "an assessment of the full context of the obligations of the employee, including the nature and seriousness of the wrongdoing, to assess whether it is reconcilable with the employment relationship."[12]

1) Misconduct Outside the Workplace

Under certain circumstances, employers are entitled to dismiss an employee for cause for misconduct not in the course of employment. The basis for the dismissal springs from a conclusion that the conduct is incompatible with continued employment. For example, the court will uphold a dismissal for cause based on an employee's absence due to being in jail.[13] Illegal conduct and conduct that compromises the employer's reputation will give rise to consideration of cause for dismissal. An employer can rely on serious criminal charges against an employee, yet for a conviction for conduct outside the workplace to justify dismissal for cause, the employer must prove on a balance of probabilities that its reputation is or will be compromised if the accused continues to be employed.[14] Ideally, employers should address conduct not tolerated and the penalty for such conduct in an employment agreement.

2) After-Acquired Cause

The concept of after-acquired cause comes into play when following an employee's dismissal not for cause, employee misconduct that would have justified dismissal for cause and that occurred before dismissal is discovered.

3) Condoned Employee Misconduct

If an employer chooses to overlook misconduct of an employee, the misconduct cannot be relied on at a later date to justify dismissal for cause. Put another way, bad deeds cannot be saved up to be used as reasons for dismissal for cause when it suits the employer to act against an employee.

E. CONSTRUCTIVE DISMISSAL — ACTIONS SPEAK LOUDER THAN WORDS

Decisions taken to realign an employee's duties and responsibilities or fine-tune working conditions without the employee's agreement can result in liability for dismissal even though the word "dismissal" is never spoken. Constructive dismissal occurs when

> an employer makes a unilateral and fundamental change to a term or condition of an employment contract without providing reasonable notice of that change to the employee. Such action amounts to a repudiation of the contract of employment by the employer whether or not he intended to continue the employment relationship. Therefore, the employee can treat the contract as wrongfully terminated and resign which, in turn, gives rise to an obligation on the employer's

part to provide damages in lieu of reasonable notice.[15]

This definition has been refined to include a series of actions that taken together demonstrate the employer no longer intends to be bound by the contract. Employers who are found to have constructively dismissed an employee are liable for termination compensation just as if the employer had terminated the employment of the employee outright.

When adjudicating a claim for constructive dismissal, the court will apply a two-step test to determine whether constructive dismissal has occurred. The court will review and interpret the facts to answer the question, Has a breach of the employment contract occurred? And if the answer is yes, then the court will consider whether the breach of contract was sufficiently important that a reasonable person in the shoes of the employee would have felt that the contract's essential terms were being substantially changed.

The obvious scenarios for constructive dismissal are demotions and compensation reductions. More subtle scenarios involve significant changes in working conditions, changes to reporting responsibility, increased or decreased working hours, significant changes to work schedule, corrective discipline suspensions, significant change in place of work, harassment, or a poisoned work environment. Constructive dismissal may be found even if compensation has not been reduced. In a recent decision of the Supreme Court of Canada, the Court held that an administrative suspension of indefinite term *with* pay amounted to constructive dismissal.[16]

Constructive dismissal can be based on a poisoned work environment. A workplace becomes poisoned for the purpose of constructive dismissal only when serious wrongful behaviour is proven. The complaining employee bears the onus of establishing a claim of poisoned workplace. A plaintiff's subjective feelings or even genuinely held beliefs are insufficient to discharge the onus of proof. There must be objective evidence.[17]

F. DISMISSAL NOT FOR CAUSE

Employees who are dismissed without cause and without notice of dismissal or pay in lieu are entitled to termination compensation mandated by the *Employment Standards Act, 2000*[18] and the common law principle of "reasonable notice."

G. FRUSTRATION OF THE EMPLOYMENT CONTRACT

Contrary to what some of my clients think, "frustration" of the employment contract is not a state of mind suffered by an employer due to the performance, or lack of it, of an employee. Frustration of a contract occurs whenever the law recognizes that without the fault of either party, "a contractual obligation has become incapable of being performed because the circumstances in which performance is called for would render it a thing radically different from that which was undertaken by the contract."[22]

In the employment context, this consideration often arises where the employee is unable to work because of a disabling illness. There is no absolute set of facts that will translate into a finding of frustration of the employment contract. Consideration is given to the length of time that the employee has been unable to work, physician's assessments of the progress of the employee's recovery, and the likelihood of the employee's being able to return to work in the foreseeable future. If the facts based on unequivocal physician opinions and including extremely lengthy absences are substantiated, an employer may be entitled to terminate the employment of an employee by relying on frustration of the employment contract. Such termination is subject to considerations of the employer's duty of accommodation under the *Human Rights Code*. And even if there are facts to justify the frustration of the employment contract, termination compensation may be payable by operation of a regulation under the *Employment Standards Act, 2000*.[23]

The possibility of frustration of contract can also arise under circumstances where the employee is unable to work due to loss of a licence that is required to perform work, as in the case of a security guard, debt collector, or registered early childhood educator, to name a few. The requirement that an employee possess and maintain a particular licence must be a bona fide occupational requirement and be identified as such in an employment agreement or offer of employment to be enforceable. The question of whether an employment contract has become frustrated must be determined by assessing the circumstances at the time of termination. A temporary loss of licence may not trigger frustration of the contract:

> The distinction is made and drawn between complete fruitlessness and mere inconvenience, hardship, loss of advantage, or the like. It

> is also necessary to differentiate a disruption that is permanent, *vis-à-vis* the contract (albeit that it may not be permanent in other respects) and one that is temporary or transient. The latter might add to the difficulties of performance. It might make performance less desirable, economically valuable, or more expensive to undertake. But it will not constitute frustration.[24]

In a case involving the dismissal of a security guard employed by a casino who could not meet new licensing requirements imposed by the *Private Security and Investigative Services Act, 2005*, which were required to maintain his eligibility for continued employment, the Ontario Divisional Court held that his employment contract had been frustrated and so would be incapable of continuation by virtue of what were at the time that the employment contract was made unforeseen legal requirements. The court observed, "To continue to bind GBH [the casino] to an employment contract, when the employee by law is prohibited from performing any services under the contract for what appears to be a lengthy and open-ended period of time, is imposing something radically different from what the parties originally agreed to."[25]

This is a very complex area of the law, and one should take legal advice before deciding to terminate employment on the basis of lengthy absence or loss of some regulatory requirement for employment. There must be some permanence to the barrier that is keeping the employee from attending work. The considerations taken into account in deciding frustration of contract due to illness are different from those taken into account in deciding frustration due to loss of licence. The *Human Rights Code* confers obligations of accommodation on employers in situations where the performance of an employee's regular duties suffers interference due to illness.

H. MISCONDUCT IN VIOLATION OF AN EXPRESS TERM OF A WRITTEN EMPLOYMENT CONTRACT — RESTRICTIVE COVENANTS

A restrictive covenant included in an employment agreement may restrain either competition or solicitation. A non-competition clause in an employment agreement restrains the departing employee from conducting business with clients or customers of his former employer, whereas a non-solicitation clause merely prohibits the departing employee from soliciting their business.[26] A covenant will be upheld only if it is reasonable in reference to the interests of the parties concerned and the interests of the public in discouraging restraints on trade.[27] If a covenant is ambiguous in the sense that what is prohibited is not clear as to activity, time, or geography, it will not be possible to demonstrate that it is reasonable.[28]

The Supreme Court of Canada has had this to say about the appropriateness of non-competition covenants: "In exceptional cases . . . the nature of the employment *may* justify a covenant prohibiting an employee not only from soliciting customers, but also from establishing his own business or working for others so as to be likely to appropriate the employer's trade connection through his acquaintance with the employer's customers."[29] In other words, the Court is not convinced of the necessity or justification for non-compete covenants in employment agreements. And if the Supreme Court of Canada is not convinced of the justification for non-compete covenants, there is a good chance that such clauses in employment contracts will not be enforced except in undefined "exceptional cases."

ENDNOTES

1 *Employment Standards Act, 2000*, SO 2000, c 41.

2 See *Movileanu v Valcom Manufacturing Group Inc*, 2007 CanLII 48989 (Ont SCJ).

3 See *Kieran v Ingram Micro Inc*, 2004 CanLII 4852 (Ont CA).

4 See *Gebreselassie v VCR Active Media Ltd*, 2007 CanLII 45710 (Ont SCJ).

5 See *Oxman v Dustbane Enterprises Ltd* (1986), 13 CCEL 209 (Ont HCJ).

6 *Employment Standards Act, 2000*, SO 2000, c 41, ss 56(1)(c) & (2).

7 *Fire Protection and Prevention Amendment Act*, SO 2011, c 13.

8 See *Termination and Severance of Employment*, O Reg 288/01, s 2(1).

9 See *McKinley v BC Tel*, 2001 SCC 38.

10 See *Plester v PolyOne Canada Inc*, 2013 ONCA 47.

11 *Dziecielski v Lighting Dimensions Inc*, 2012 ONSC 1877 at para 39, quoting Randall Scott Echlin & Matthew LO Certosimo, *Just Cause: The Law of Summary Dismissal in Canada* (Aurora, ON: Canada Law Book, 1998) (loose-leaf 2011 supplement) at para 13:210.

12 *Wilson v Legacy Private Trust*, 2014 ONSC 2070 at para 111.

13 See *Quebec (Commission des droits de la personne et des droits de la jeunesse) v Maksteel Québec Inc*, 2003 SCC 68.

14 See *Kelly v Linamar Corporation*, 2005 CanLII 42487 (Ont SCJ).

15 Quoted in *Farber v Royal Trust Co*, 1997 CanLII 387 at para 34 (SCC).

16 *Potter v New Brunswick Legal Aid Services Commission*, 2015 SCC 10.

17 See *General Motors of Canada Limited v Johnson*, 2013 ONCA 502.

18 Except for construction employees: see *Scapillati v A Potvin Construction Ltd*, 1997 CanLII 12420 (Ont Ct Gen Div). But denial of *Employment Standards Act, 2000* benefits does not deprive non-union construction workers of common law remedies.

19 *Gristey v Emke Schaab Climatecare Inc*, 2014 ONSC 1798.

20 See *Di Tomaso v Crown Metal Packaging Canada LP*, 2011 ONCA 469.

21 *Markoulakis v SNC-Lavalin Inc*, 2015 ONSC 1081.

22 *Duong v Linamar Corporation*, 2010 ONSC 3159 at para 33.

23 *Termination and Severance of Employment*, O Reg 288/01, ss 2(3) and 9(2)(b).

24 *Cowie v Great Blue Heron Charity Casino*, 2011 ONSC 6357 at para 23 (Div Ct), quoting GHL Fridman, *The Law of Contract in Canada*, 4th ed (Scarborough, ON: Carswell, 1999) at 679–80.

25 *Cowie v Great Blue Heron Charity Casino*, 2011 ONSC 6357 at para 34 (Div Ct).

26 See *HL Staebler Company Limited v Allan*, 2008 ONCA 576.

27 See *Elsley v JG Collins Ins Agencies*, 1978 CanLII 7 (SCC).

28 See *Martin v ConCreate USL Limited Partnership*, 2013 ONCA 72.

29 *Elsley v JG Collins Ins Agencies*, 1978 CanLII 7 at 926 (SCC) [emphasis added].

A dismissed employee who believes that she has been unfairly compensated in the termination of her employment may choose to commence an action (lawsuit) in Small Claims Court or the Superior Court of Justice, file an application (complaint) under the *Human Rights Code*[3] with the Human Rights Tribunal of Ontario, or file a complaint with the Ministry of Labour under the *Employment Standards Act, 2000*. At common law, claimants must commence an action for damages for wrongful dismissal within two years of being dismissed. If they fail to meet this limitation period, the claim will be statute barred. Different limitation periods apply for remedies under the *Human Rights Code* and the *Employment Standards Act, 2000*. The choice of forum will depend on the nature of the remedy and the amount of damages sought.

A. SMALL CLAIMS COURT

Small Claims Court is a branch of the Superior Court of Justice. The monetary jurisdiction of the Small Claims Court is capped at $25,000 plus legal costs. The court has no jurisdiction to reinstate a dismissed employee to employment, which is to be contrasted with the authority of the Human Rights Tribunal of Ontario and the Ontario Labour Relations Board. The Small Claims Court has been referred to as a court for self-help, providing a forum for the resolution of low-value claims arising out of disputes over debts, property loss, or property damage. The monetary jurisdiction of the court has evolved over time from claims up to $1,000 in 1993 (except in Metropolitan Toronto, where it was $3,000), to $10,000 in 2000 and $25,000 as of 2010. Litigants may be self-represented, or, alternatively, representation may be through lawyers, paralegals, or articling students. With the range of complexities in employment law, it is unwise for a defendant to be self-represented.

Proceedings in the Small Claims Court begin with issuing a claim, which may be challenged by issuing a defence. The defence has to be served on the plaintiff personally or by mail, courier, fax, or alternative service as allowed by the *Rules of the Small Claims Court*[4] within twenty days from the date of being served with the claim, and after that the defence has to be filed with the court with proof of service on the plaintiff. The claim and the defence must be prepared using Small Claims Court forms available online at the court's website.[5] A filing fee of $75 is payable at the time of filing a claim or defendant's claim (counterclaim), and $40 is payable at the time of filing a defence. If a defendant forgets or otherwise fails to serve and file a defence, the plaintiff may note the defendant in default and obtain judgment for the amounts claimed without giving the defendant another say in the claim. At the time of filing the defence, all documents that the defendant intends to rely on must also be filed. Unlike proceedings in the Superior Court of Justice, there is no examination for discovery, where documents are presented and examined.

The next step is a settlement conference, which is conducted by a referee. Persons appointed by the government to be referees do not have to have any legal training, and, in fact, most do not. This reality can be frustrating for professionally trained representatives. Sometimes a deputy judge will conduct a settlement conference, but it is not common. Before a settlement conference, both parties must exchange any documents not already disclosed that they intend to rely on to prove their claim or defence, and both parties must disclose the names of their witnesses, if any. The purpose of the settlement conference, as the name suggests, is to resolve the dispute, but the parties are under no obligation to reach a settlement. If the claim is not settled at the settlement conference, it will be listed for trial after the plaintiff pays a $100 court fee.

B. SUPERIOR COURT OF JUSTICE

A litigant in the Superior Court of Justice may elect to proceed by way of simplified procedure or regular track. A simplified procedure claim cannot exceed $100,000 plus legal costs, but the procedure provides a faster vehicle for reaching a trial date, assuming the matter cannot be settled.

A party commences a court action by issuing a statement of claim, serving it on the defendant, and paying a filing fee of $181 at the Superior Court of Justice. The defendant must file a statement of defence in return within thirty days provided that a notice of intent to defend has been filed and that the filing fee of $144 has been paid to the court. The plaintiff can also file a reply to the defence. Note that a claim for wrongful dismissal may also include a claim for damages for a violation of the *Human Rights Code* if that claim can be framed as an actionable wrong separate from the claim for damages for breach of the employment contract.

The next steps are delivery of an affidavit of documents by each party to the other party and an examination for discovery, at which the plaintiff accompanied by a lawyer must attend to answer questions under oath or affirmation that are asked by the defendant's lawyer. A transcript is made of the questions and answers. The process then repeats itself with the plaintiff's lawyer questioning a representative of the defendant. The simplified procedure differs from the regular track by requiring the parties to include the names and addresses of persons who may have knowledge of the matters in dispute in the affidavits of documents. In addition, examination for discovery under the simplified procedure is limited to a maximum of two hours per witness.

If the matter is not settled at or after examination for discovery, the matter proceeds to the next step, mandatory mediation, which requires the parties to exchange written briefs outlining their positions and the justifications of those positions in law. The briefs are filed with the mediator and are the focus of the mediation meeting. The mediator is usually chosen on consent, if possible, and if agreement is not possible, one of the parties can apply to the court to have a mediator appointed. Mediation is not a hearing, and the mediator has no authority to make the parties agree on a settlement.

If the claim cannot be settled at mediation, it proceeds to a pretrial conference held before a master or judge. The parties must file a pretrial conference memorandum outlining the same issues disclosed in their mediation briefs. The presiding court official at the pretrial conference will attempt to persuade the parties of the relative strengths and weaknesses of their positions with a view to getting a settlement. If a settlement cannot be achieved, the matter will be scheduled for trial after a trial record has been filed and after the $337 filing fee has been paid.

C. DAMAGES (SHOW ME THE MONEY)

There is a range of damages that can be claimed in wrongful dismissal lawsuits. The primary damages that are claimed are damages for pay in lieu of reasonable notice, which are based on a calculation of "global" compensation multiplied by the claimed notice period. Global compensation is the total of an employee's base pay plus bonus, commissions, profit-sharing, if any, and any perks including, for example, pension, car allowance, health care benefits, and share purchase options, if any.

1) Aggravated Damages

Aggravated damages are compensatory damages. They compensate a plaintiff for the additional harm suffered because of the way that the contract was breached.[6] In a claim for damages for wrongful dismissal, aggravated damages may be awarded because of the employer's unfair or bad-faith conduct in the course of the dismissal.

Damages for future loss of income can be claimed and are awarded where the employee has not recovered from the effects of the employer's actions and where the employee has suffered a loss of earning capacity because of tortious (civilly wrong) conduct by the employer. The normal distress and hurt feelings resulting from dismissal are not compensable. But if an employee can prove that the manner of dismissal caused mental distress that was within contemplation of the parties, those damages will be awarded not through an arbitrary extension of the notice period but through an award reflecting the actual damages.[7] Employer conduct that could attract such damages includes the following:

- attacking an employee's reputation by statements made at the time of dismissal
- misrepresentation regarding the reason for dismissal
- dismissal crafted to deprive an employee of pension benefits or some other right

2) Punitive Damages

Punitive damages may be awarded against an employer in a wrongful dismissal action if the plaintiff can establish two requirements:

- The employer's conduct was malicious, oppressive, high-handed, and a marked departure from ordinary standards of decent behaviour.
- An award of punitive damages is rationally required to punish the employer and to meet the objectives of retribution, deterrence, and denunciation.

3) Intentional Infliction of Mental Suffering

A plaintiff may also seek damages based on the employer's inappropriate conduct by advancing a tort claim for intentional infliction of mental suffering. To succeed, the plaintiff must prove that the employer's conduct was all of the following:

- flagrant and outrageous
- calculated to harm the plaintiff
- the cause of the plaintiff's suffering a visible and provable illness[8]

If a plaintiff makes a "rule 49 offer to settle" before trial, if the defendant does not accept the offer, and if the plaintiff wins and is awarded an amount equal to or greater than the offer, the court can award the plaintiff substantial indemnity costs from the date that the offer was made. Conversely, if a defendant makes a rule 49 offer to settle before trial and if the plaintiff wins but is awarded an amount equal to or less than the offer, the defendant, even though the loser, can ask to have partial indemnity costs awarded against the plaintiff from the date that the offer was made.

1) Costs in Small Claims Court

Costs awarded in Small Claims Court are capped at 15 percent of the amount claimed unless the court can be persuaded to penalize a party or a party's representative for unreasonable behaviour in the proceeding. If the successful party is represented by a lawyer or a paralegal, a representation fee may be awarded at the discretion of the court, but the amount will be nominal. Reasonable disbursement expenses can also be awarded.

ENDNOTES

1 *Employment Standards Act, 2000*, SO 2000, c 41.
2 Hon Justice John R Sproat, *Wrongful Dismissal Handbook*, 4th ed (Toronto: Thomson Carswell, 2006) at 2-1.
3 *Human Rights Code*, RSO 1990, c H.19.
4 Ontario, *Rules of the Small Claims Court*, O Reg 258/98, r 8.03(1).
5 Online: *Ontario Court Services* www.ontariocourtforms.on.ca/english/scc/.
6 See *Boucher v Wal-Mart Canada Corp*, 2014 ONCA 419.
7 See *Honda Canada Inc v Keays*, 2008 SCC 39.
8 See *Boucher v Wal-Mart Canada Corp*, 2014 ONCA 419.
9 See Chapter 12, Section A for more information.
10 See Chapter 8 for more information.
11 Online: *Ontario Labour Relations Board* www.olrb.gov.on.ca/english/bdocs.htm.
12 Ontario, *Rules of Civil Procedure*, RRO 1990, Reg 194.
13 Ontario, *Rules of the Small Claims Court*, O Reg 258/98.

CHAPTER NINETEEN

Union Employment Relationship

What You Should Know

If your business becomes unionized, you will face the following:

- loss of ability to manage the enterprise according to your values and vision
- loss of ability to recognize and reward individual employees for their contributions to the enterprise
- loss of ability to motivate and encourage excellence through profit-sharing or a bonus system (such initiatives are permitted only with union approval)
- second-guessing by the union of employee-promotion decisions
- limitation of ability, almost to the point of impossibility, to terminate employment for substandard performance or even to criticize performance or conduct
- loss of ability to respond to economic pressures on or to preserve the viability of your business without the approval of the union
- prohibition of individual employment contracts

A. THE COLLECTIVE BARGAINING REGIME

In Ontario, the *Labour Relations Act, 1995* (***LRA***)[1] sets rules for the following:

- unionization of employees (certification)
- negotiation and content of collective agreements

- termination of union representation (decertification)
- definition of unfair labour practices (e.g., coercion and intimidation)
- termination of employment arbitration
- determination of liability for the continuation of existing collective bargaining relationships after the sale of a business

Rules relating to the unionization of employees in a federally regulated business are set out in the *Canada Labour Code*.[2]

B. ONTARIO LABOUR RELATIONS BOARD

The Ontario Labour Relations Board **(OLRB)** administers and interprets the *LRA*. The Board's adjudicative function is carried out through hearings presided over by a one-person panel or a three-person panel consisting of a neutral vice-chair, a union representative, and an employer representative, but more often than not a hearing will be conducted by a vice-chair sitting alone. The provincial government appoints all Board members through orders in council. The Board is an administrative tribunal, not a court of record, and this means that there is no transcript of Board proceedings.

A field services department staffed by labour relations officers and labour relations specialists assists the OLRB in its adjudicative function. The primary functions of the field services department are as follows:

- to attempt to assist parties to resolve the dispute that brought them to the Board
- to arrange and preside over union certification and decertification votes
- to provide conciliation services in appeals under the *Employment Standards Act, 2000*
- to provide conciliation services in applications under the *Occupational Health and Safety Act* that allege an employee has been subjected to reprisals for exercising rights under that Act or its regulations
- to provide conciliation services in appeals by employers regarding orders of health and safety inspectors

A party wishing to engage in proceedings under the *LRA* must properly select and prepare one or more forms, of over 177, specifically drafted by the OLRB for the subject of the party's dispute or request. Proceedings before the Board are governed by its *Rules of Procedure*,[3] and Board decisions are based on the credibility of testifying witnesses, the documents produced, the Board's interpretation of the *LRA*, and previously decided cases. The Board's website provides access to its *Rules of Procedure*, information bulletins, forms, and prior caselaw.[4]

C. UNION ORGANIZING CAMPAIGNS

All bargaining units must have a minimum of two employees to be eligible for a union certification application. Note that the construction and the non-construction industries are governed by separate and distinct procedural rules for applying for unionization and termination of union representation.

The *LRA* defines "construction industry" as businesses "engaged in constructing, altering, decorating, repairing or demolishing buildings, structures, roads, sewers, water or gas mains, pipe lines, tunnels, bridges, canals or other works at the site."[5] But this definition is not determinative for identifying a business as a construction-industry business. The OLRB looks at the work performed and applies a two-part test:

- Is the work performed on a construction site?
- Is the work necessary and integral to the work on that site?

In its analysis, the Board will consider the context in which the work is performed and how integrated, if at all, the activities of the target business's employees are with the construction work that goes on at the site. Operating concrete-pumping trucks at a construction site is deemed to be work integrated with the construction work at the site, and therefore work in the construction industry. On the other hand, delivery of concrete mix or other materials to a job site is not deemed to be work in the construction industry.

1) Certification Process

In general, unions win the right to represent employees and be their bargaining agent by soliciting non-managerial employees to sign union membership cards. Professional union organizers have no right to be on a target employer's property to promote the union. And for anyone to promote the union or solicit employees to sign up for membership during working hours on the employer's property is against the law.

b) Common Mistakes That Employers Make

The following are common mistakes that employers make causing them to miss the deadline for filing a response to a certification application:

- allowing the office fax machine to run out of paper and not refilling it until after the two-day deadline to reply has passed
- waiting until the employer's lawyer returns from vacation before responding to the application
- allowing the envelope with the application to sit in the boss's in-basket while he is away on vacation
- where the owner's home address is listed as the business's head office, allowing the envelope with the application to sit in the owner's home mailbox while she is away on vacation

Small businesses are particularly vulnerable to the strict time limits because of a lack of office administration infrastructure.

c) Response to Certification Application

Assuming that an employer files a response to the application within the two-day time limit, challenges, if warranted, can be made to the following:

- the number of employees that the union states were working in the bargaining unit on the application date
- the counting of managerial employees as bargaining unit employees
- the existence of locations where the union claims employees are performing work
- the work performed as non-bargaining unit work
- the description of the bargaining unit
- the jurisdiction of the OLRB

Ultimately, the OLRB will decide the appropriateness of the bargaining unit applied for. Should the total number of employees at work on the application date be in fact greater than that estimated by the union, the application may be defeated. This happens when the total number of cards signed is less than 40 percent of the actual total number of employees at work in the bargaining unit on the application date.

d) When a Vote Is Required and Setting the Vote Date and Voters' List

There is a popular misconception that unionizing a business in Ontario requires the OLRB to conduct a secret ballot vote, with eligible employees of a business voting to accept or reject the union's application to be their representative. Unfortunately this is not true.

A secret ballot vote is mandatory if the target business is a non-construction-industry business. If, on the other hand, the target business is a construction-industry business, the union has the choice of applying for a secret ballot vote or applying on the basis of the number of signed union membership cards collected. Construction-industry unions rarely test their support by asking the Board to hold a secret ballot vote. Construction-industry union certification may be automatic, without a vote, if the union can submit membership cards from more than 55 percent of the employees in the intended bargaining unit. It is within the Board's discretion to order a secret ballot vote even if the union submits membership cards from more than 55 percent of the employees in the intended bargaining unit, but this rarely happens and mostly depends on successfully persuading the Board that employees were misled or confused when they signed the union membership cards.[7] If the union submits membership cards from at least 40 percent but not more than 55 percent of the employees in the intended bargaining unit, the Board must order a secret ballot vote.[8] If the union files membership evidence from fewer than 40 percent of the employees in the intended bargaining unit, the application will be dismissed.[9]

If a secret ballot vote is required, the OLRB will set a date and time for the vote and determine the voter constituency. The date of the vote will be within five days of the date that the certification application was filed on, but in the case of the construction industry, the vote will be five days after the date on which the application was delivered to the employer or the date on which the application was filed with the Board whichever is later.

e) Before the Vote

Up until the vote takes place, the employer and the union can campaign to persuade employees to reject or support the union. How an employer manages the business during an organizing campaign is closely scrutinized by the OLRB. Changes to hours of work, schedules, or work assignments and discipline of any kind, to name only a few examples, will be viewed with great suspicion and could be subject to censure by the Board.

Dismissals during an organizing campaign are repeatedly the subject of unfair labour practice applications, with the union alleging retaliation against the disciplined employee because he was allegedly a key union organizer or a major supporter of the union. Where the Board is persuaded of the truth of the union's allegations, it will order the employee reinstated with back pay and interest. When responding to unfair labour practice applications, employers are required to prove that they are innocent of the alleged wrongdoings, which is the opposite of the normal evidentiary burden where an accused is innocent until proven guilty.

What employers say during the organizing campaign and the manner of their response to it is scrutinized by the Board. It is permissible to urge employees to reject the union, but during the five-day period leading up to the vote, employers cannot make promises to enhance working conditions or compensation. Also mandatory attendance meetings held to promote the employer's perspective are prohibited. Threats of any kind made by a member of management or any person acting on behalf of management, whether authorized to speak or not, to encourage a vote against the union will be challenged by the union with an unfair labour practice application. If the union is successful, the Board can disqualify the results of the vote and order another vote. In extreme cases of proven employer interference, the Board will impose certification regardless of the vote's outcome.[10]

Frequently employees believe that if they have signed a union membership card, they must vote in favour of the union at the certification vote. That is not true. All eligible voters are free to vote for or against the union regardless of whether they signed or did not sign a union membership card.

Union intimidation of employees will also be censured, but such acts are generally hard to prove, and rules for campaigning imposed on the union are less stringent. The union is allowed to and will promise wage increases and sweeping improvements to working conditions. It will omit to tell employees that changes to their wages or working conditions can be achieved only through the negotiation of such changes as part of a collective agreement. And as far as the Board is concerned, this is regarded as salesmanship, not as unfair practice.

f) The Vote

In the non-construction industry, all employees in the voting constituency determined by the OLRB, who had an employment relationship[11] with the employer on the date of the certification application, are eligible to vote. While in the construction industry, only those employees who were employed, at work, and doing bargaining unit work at a job site on the date of the certification application will be allowed to vote. Persons who were laid off or not working on the application date are not considered employees in the bargaining unit for the purpose of an application for certification or decertification.

The vote is conducted by a Board officer. The employer and the union are each allowed to have one representative present as scrutineer. A voters' list is compiled in consultation with the employer and the union, and any person that either party claims should be on the voters' list is listed with any challenges by the other party noted. At the vote, it is up to the individual scrutineers to challenge the eligibility of persons requesting a ballot. Any person challenged is allowed to vote, but her ballot is segregated. Initially, the unchallenged ballots are counted, and after that if the addition of challenged ballots could impact the outcome of the vote, the Board will hold a hearing to receive submissions on the eligibility of each challenged voter. If a voter is ruled eligible, his ballot is then counted.

Normally, the vote is held at the employer's premises and often in a lunchroom. However, the Board has the authority to hold the vote outside the workplace, electronically, or by phone.

A majority of the ballots cast plus one determines the outcome of the vote, and a tie vote defeats the application. It is important to remember that in a voting constituency of one hundred voters if only ten employees vote and if of these ten employees six vote in favour of the union, the business will be unionized notwithstanding the fact that 90 percent of the eligible voters failed to express their wish.

When unions lose a certification vote, it is not uncommon for them to file an unfair labour practice complaint alleging that the employer coerced or intimidated the voting employees into voting against the union. In this situation, a hearing will be convened before the Board, and the employer will need to persuade it on the balance of probabilities that the allegations of coercion and intimidation are not true. Otherwise the Board can and will disqualify the results of the vote.

Finally, if the union loses the vote, a one-year bar to filing an application to represent the same employees is imposed.

2) Collective Agreement Negotiations

Once the OLRB certifies the union to be the exclusive bargaining agent for the employees, the union will issue a notice to bargain to the employer. The employer then has a duty to meet with the union and try to

is appointed and certain time limits expire.[16] This quarantine has been referred to as the "freeze period," and the Board has interpreted it as a requirement to preserve a "pattern of employment" that gives the union the protection of negotiating the first agreement from a starting point of the status quo.

This restriction is a challenge for employers, who must respond to economic changes and market pressures. It makes it possible for the union to dictate to the employer matters relating to the economic viability or, in the extreme, survival of the business. Layoffs implemented during the freeze period are almost always attacked by the union with an unfair labour practice complaint that imputes to the employer some anti-union strategy aimed at weakening the employees' resolve to continue to support their new bargaining representative.

If the employer and the union are unable to reach an agreement, either party may file a request for the assistance of a conciliation officer in the negotiations. And after the parties have met at least once under the auspices of the conciliation officer, either party can end the negotiations by requesting a "no-board" report from the conciliation officer. The request cannot be refused. The no-board report is a letter issued by the conciliation officer confirming that the parties have been unable to reach agreement on a collective agreement and that a board of mediation is not recommended, hence the name no board. The issuance of a no-board report is a formality that starts the clock running toward strike or lock-out action, if so desired.

Fourteen days after the date of the no-board report, the parties are free to engage in so-called economic warfare: the union may withdraw the services of its members and start a strike, and the employer may lock out its employees. An alternative to a strike or a lock-out, where the parties have been unable to achieve a first collective agreement, is binding arbitration.[17]

D. TERMINATING BARGAINING RIGHTS — DECERTIFICATION

1) Non-construction-Industry Termination by Employees

The procedure for termination of bargaining rights by employees in a non-construction industry is complicated and daunting for a layperson. Knowledge of section 63 of the *LRA* and rule 10 of the OLRB's *Rules of Procedure* as well as the Board's thirteen-page Information Bulletin No 2 is required to successfully file an application.[18] The employees cannot have any assistance or encouragement from management, and evidence of management's participation, which includes retaining lawyers on behalf of the employees, will defeat the application.

The employees must complete Board Form A-6, "Application for Termination of Bargaining Rights Under Section 63 of the Act," Form C-3, "Notice to Union of Application for Termination of Bargaining Rights Under Section 63 of the Act," and Form A-9, "Declaration Verifying Evidence of Employee Wishes."[19] A document that is signed and dated by each employee who supports the application and that states explicitly in writing that the employees do not want to be represented by the union must accompany Form A-6 when it is filed with the Board.

The steps that must be taken to give notice to the union of the application to terminate bargaining rights are more onerous than the steps that the union must take to deliver a certification application to the employer. The termination application must be delivered to "the most senior union official responsible for the bargaining unit." This contrasts sharply with the procedure for giving notice of a certification application to an employer, which allows for delivery to any representative of the employer. Correct identification of "the most senior union official responsible for the bargaining unit" and the corresponding address or fax number can prove challenging. The termination application must also be delivered to the employer, but the Board's *Rules of Procedure* do not specify any particular person for delivery.

The application must then be filed with the Board no later than two days after delivery of the termination application to the union and the employer. Failure to meet this deadline will result in the Board's termination of the application.

2) Construction-Industry Decertification by Employees

Decertifications by construction-industry employees are even more complicated than non-construction-industry decertifications due to ICI-sector province-wide agreements and procedures mandated by the *LRA*.

Since 20 May 2015, employees of a bargaining unit may apply to decertify the union after the commencement of the last two months of the operation of a three-year collective agreement. In the case of a collective agreement of more than three years, the employees of a bargaining unit may apply after the commencement of the thirty-fifth month of its operation and before the commencement of the thirty-seventh month of its operation.

E. PURCHASER CONSIDERATIONS IN THE SALE OF A UNIONIZED BUSINESS

The bargaining rights of a union representing the employees of a business that is sold are extensively protected under the *LRA*. The OLRB interprets this protection as covering the activities and the work performed by the employees of the unionized business.

The *LRA* states, "Where an employer who is bound by or is a party to a collective agreement with a trade union or council of trade unions *sells* his, her or its *business*, the person to whom the business has been sold is, until the Board otherwise declares, bound by the collective agreement as if the person had been a party thereto . . . ."[20] "Business" is defined as including "a part or parts thereof," and "sells" as including "leases, *transfers* and any other manner of disposition, and 'sold' and 'sale' have corresponding meanings."[21] The Board has added that "[t]he word *transfers* . . . is capable of describing a multitude of transactions whether by sale, exchange, gift, trust or otherwise by which property, rights, or interests, etc. are transmitted absolutely, conditionally etc. or by operation of law from one person to another."[22] If the work performed by the employees after the transfer (transaction) is substantially the same as before the transfer and if the work is being performed by the same employees, there is a strong case for finding that there has been a sale of the business for the purposes of the *LRA*.

There is no statutory definition of "business" in the *LRA*, and it is within the Board's exclusive jurisdiction to consider the facts of each impugned transaction and to provide its opinion on what the transaction delivered. Decisions of the Board have expressed the following view:

> a business is 'the totality of the undertaking.' The physical assets of buildings, tools and equipment used in a business are not necessarily the undertaking *per se* but are, along with management and operating personnel and their skills, necessary in the operations to fulfill the obligations undertaken with a hope of producing profit to assume its success. The total of these things along with certain intangibles such as goodwill constitute a business.[23]

The Board's assessment will focus on the substance rather than the form of the transaction. Can it be said that a "dynamic activity," a "going concern," or a "functional economic vehicle" has been transferred? If so, the purchaser will be bound by the existing collective agreement terms and conditions, including wage rates, negotiated by the union and the vendor (predecessor) of the business. There is no template that can be applied to any given set of facts to assess the risk of a Board determination that the components of a transaction constitute a business or part of a business, with union bargaining rights attached.

F. TERMINATION OF EMPLOYMENT AND ARBITRATION

Unionized employees in Ontario have no common law rights of action in the courts against their employer for breach of any of the terms of their employment relationship. The employment contract for unionized employees is the collective agreement negotiated on their behalf by their bargaining agent as certified by the OLRB.

All collective agreements in Ontario are required by law to have dispute resolution clauses, more commonly known as grievance/arbitration clauses. Any disputes about how the collective agreement is administered by management, including those relating to working conditions or discipline and discharge of employees, must be resolved according to the prescribed grievance/arbitration procedure. The mandated procedure ordinarily includes a series of steps that start with bringing written disclosure of the grievance to the attention of management within set time limits followed by a response from management and then meetings with a view to resolving the dispute without arbitration.

If settlement cannot be achieved, the dissatisfied party files a notice of arbitration with the other party, and an attempt is made to agree on the selection of an arbitrator. Failing agreement, an arbitrator will be appointed by the Ontario Ministry of Labour. An arbitrator's authority (jurisdiction) to decide the dispute comes from the negotiated terms of the collective agreement. Arbitration hearings are conducted like court trials but without the formality and the rigid rules for the receipt of evidence. Arbitrators appointed under the terms of a collective agreement have exclusive jurisdiction with regard to all the disputes or differences that arise from the collective agreement.[24] With regards to dismissal grievances, employers must prove "just cause" to sustain a dismissal. If sufficient proof

A struck employer can restrain such activities by going to court to request an injunction. But the Court of Appeal for Ontario has had this to say about the availability of injunctions in a labour dispute: "Strikes and the picket lines that go with them are evolving human dramas where risks of property damage, personal injury or obstruction of lawful entry are best controlled by flexible and even-handed policing. Only where this fails should the court, with its blunt instrument of the injunction, be resorted to."[32] Unfortunately, this point of view anticipates that the police will take responsibility and play an active role in maintaining the peace in labour disputes, a role that the police are not always enthusiastic to play.

Striking employees have the right to reinstatement to their jobs, if they make an unconditional application in writing within six months from the commencement of a lawful strike unless:

- the employer no longer has persons engaged in performing work of the same or similar nature to the kind of work the employee performed prior to the employee's cessation of work; or
- there has been a suspension or discontinuance for cause of an employer's operations, or any part thereof.

It is a violation of the *LRA* to discharge or discipline an employee in a bargaining unit without just cause during the period that begins on the date on which a strike or lock-out became lawful and that ends on the earlier of the date on which a new collective agreement is entered into and the date on which the trade union no longer represents the employees in the bargaining unit.[33]

It is also a violation of the *LRA* for a union to go on strike during the life of a collective agreement or for an employer to lock out unionized workers. As an alternative to seeking an injunction, employers affected by an illegal strike may file an application for a cease and desist order with the OLRB.

Best Business Practices

- Treat employees with dignity and respect.
- Compensate employees fairly.
- Support the well-being of employees through affordable health care coverage.
- Set policies and standards of performance that are fair and attainable.

- Publicize workplace policies and apply those policies consistently and even-handedly.
- Provide an employee manual that discloses management's expectations for workplace conduct and performance.
- Lead by example.
- Avoid favouritism in setting pay for and providing privileges to family members.
- Maintain regular communication of your vision, values, and expectations.

ENDNOTES

1 *Labour Relations Act, 1995*, SO 1995, c 1, Schedule A.

2 *Canada Labour Code*, RSC 1985, c L-2.

3 Ontario Labour Relations Board, *Rules of Procedure* (Toronto: OLRB, July 2014), online: www.olrb.gov.on.ca/english/bdocs.htm.

4 Online: *Ontario Labour Relations Board* www.olrb.gov.on.ca.

5 *Labour Relations Act, 1995*, SO 1995, c 1, Schedule A, s 1(1).

6 *International Brotherhood of Electrical Workers, Local 353 v Synapse Electric Limited*, 2013 CanLII 82268 at para 26 (OLRB) [emphasis added].

7 See *Labour Relations Act, 1995*, SO 1995, c 1, Schedule A, s 128.1(13).

8 See *Labour Relations Act, 1995*, SO 1995, c 1, Schedule A, s 128.1(12).

9 See *Labour Relations Act, 1995*, SO 1995, c 1, Schedule A, s 128.1(7).

10 See *Labour Relations Act, 1995*, SO 1995, c 1, Schedule A, s 11.

11 In the nonconstruction industry, employees who were absent on the certification application date due to maternity leave, sick leave, vacation, layoff, or injury reported to the Ontario Workplace Safety and Insurance Board are allowed to vote.

12 See *Labour Relations Act, 1995*, SO 1995, c 1, Schedule A, s 15.

13 *Labour Relations Act, 1995*, SO 1995, c 1, Schedule A, s 126(1).

14 *Labour Relations Act, 1995*, SO 1995, c 1, Schedule A, s 45.

15 *Pine Ridge District Health Unit*, [1977] OLRB Rep Feb 65 at para 14.

16 See *Labour Relations Act, 1995*, SO 1995, c 1, Schedule A, s 86(1).

17 *Labour Relations Act, 1995*, SO 1995, c 1, Schedule A, s 43.

18 *Labour Relations Act, 1995*, SO 1995, c 1, Schedule A, s 63; Ontario Labour Relations Board, *Rules of Procedure* (July 2014), online: www.olrb.gov.on.ca/english/bdocs.htm; Ontario Labour Relations Board, Information

Bulletin No 2, "Termination of Bargaining Rights Under Section 63 of the *Labour Relations Act*" (October 2014), online: www.olrb.gov.on.ca/english/iblist.htm.

19 Online: *Ontario Labour Relations Board* www.olrb.gov.on.ca/english/FormsNum.htm.

20 *Labour Relations Act, 1995*, SO 1995, c 1, Schedule A, s 69(2) [emphasis added].

21 *Labour Relations Act, 1995*, SO 1995, c 1, Schedule A, s 69(1) [emphasis added].

22 *Thorco Mfg Ltd* (1965), 65 CLLC at para 16,052.

23 *Canadian Union of Public Employees v Metropolitan Parking Inc*, 1979 CanLII 815 at para 29 (OLRB).

24 See *Weber v Ontario Hydro*, 1995 CanLII 108 (SCC).

25 Quoted in Vanessa Lu, "CP Rail to Fight Order to Hire Back Engineer Who Used Cocaine" *Toronto Star* (17 July 2014), online: www.thestar.com/business/2014/07/17/cp_rail_to_fight_order_to_hire_back_engineer_who_used_cocaine.html.

26 *Canadian Pacific Railway v Teamsters Canada Rail Conference*, 2014 CanLII 51686 (Can Railway Office of Arbitration & Dispute Resolution).

27 *Canadian Pacific Railway v Teamsters Canada Rail Conference*, 2014 CanLII 51686 (Can Railway Office of Arbitration & Dispute Resolution).

28 *Teamsters Canada Rail Conference v Canadian Pacific Railway Company*, 2017 QCCA 479.

29 See Section C(2)(b), above in this chapter.

30 See *RWDSU, Local 558 v Pepsi-Cola Canada Beverages (West) Ltd*, 2002 SCC 8.

31 *RWDSU, Local 558 v Pepsi-Cola Canada Beverages (West) Ltd*, 2002 SCC 8.

32 *Industrial Hardwood Products (1996) Ltd v International Wood and Allied Workers of Canada, Local 2693*, 2001 CanLII 24071 at para 16 (Ont CA).

33 *Labour Relations Act, 1995*, SO 1995, Schedule A, s 80.1(1).

CHAPTER TWENTY

Closing Comments

The employment relationship is complex, impacted by human nature, workplace laws and regulations, court decisions, and administrative tribunal policy interpretations and applications. Forty years' experience before the courts and workplace tribunals have informed and reinforced one simple principle of workplace management in the writer: management policies will not be enforced by adjudicators unless those policies are reasonable, transparent, in writing, communicated, and even-handedly applied to all members of the workforce. The preceding pages are an attempt to give the layperson entrepreneur or business owner a "heads-up" insight into basic Ontario workplace laws and the interpretation of those laws by the courts and workplace administrative tribunals, with a view to raising awareness of the parameters of workplace management. Mistakes in employee management can be extremely costly in terms of money, time, and morale. Proactive management of the workforce is mandatory for a successful business.

dismissal not for cause. *See* not-for-cause dismissal.

divisional Court. One or three judges of the Ontario Superior Court of Justice sitting as appellate judges of an application for judicial review of a court or workplace administrative tribunal decision.

duty of fidelity. In the employment context, implied term of an employment contract requiring an employee to act in the best interests of her employer.

duty to mitigate damages. Duty of a terminated employee to diligently and expeditiously try to become re-employed.

examination for discovery. Step in a lawsuit following the delivery of the statement of claim, statement of defence, and affidavits of documents that is intended to provide detailed information about the alleged facts recorded in the statements of claim and defence. The plaintiff must appear in person and answer questions from the opposing party's lawyers. Similarly, the defendant or a representative of a corporate defendant must attend for the same purpose. A transcript of the questions and answers is made.

injunction. Court order commonly referred to as an extraordinary remedy because it is an order to stop a defendant from continuing the conduct complained of or to compel the defendant to take some specific action before a full trial on the merits of the matter has been conducted. Injunctions in a labour context are requested to stop union picket lines from blockading ingress to and egress from an employer's premises during a strike.

jurisdiction. Power or authority to make a decision or to issue an order.

mediation. Mandatory event for the purpose of attempting to reach settlement of a lawsuit commenced in the Ontario Superior Court of Justice. Mediation is conducted by a person who is either agreed to by the parties or imposed by the court when the parties cannot agree. The mediator has no power to make the parties agree on a settlement.

not-for-cause dismissal. Termination of employment without blameworthy conduct, which violates an employment agreement.

plaintiff. Person who initiates a lawsuit, asking the court to grant a remedy for the defendant's alleged wrongful acts.

prescribed duties. Duties defined by statute.

probationary term. Time specifically stated in an employment contract that employers use to assess a new hire's suitability for a job. The Ontario *Employment Standards Act, 2000* sets a period of three months as the maximum time for this assessment. If the new hire is dismissed during this time frame, no termination compensation will be owing unless the dismissal was in bad faith. Employers may choose a longer time, but if the employee's employment is terminated beyond the three-month limit, termination compensation will be owed.

release. In the employment context, document signed by an employee in settlement of all disputes arising out of his employment in which he promises not to commence any proceedings in the courts or before a workplace administrative tribunal in consideration of receiving money from his former employer. As a note of caution, if the employee does not get independent legal advice before signing the release, a court may nullify it.

reply. In the context of the litigation process, document filed by the plaintiff that responds to certain allegations in the statement of defence.

statement of claim. Story of the plaintiff's reasons for asking the court to rule on the outlined dispute and the remedy sought, for example, money or a declaration.

statement of defence. Reasons that the defendant refuses to do what the plaintiff asks, or to give the plaintiff what is requested.

statute. Law passed by the Parliament of Canada or one of the provinces.

swear an information. To make a written complaint under oath stating that you have reason to believe that a person or business has committed an offence referenced in the information.

termination compensation. Money paid to an employee whose employment was terminated not for cause. It includes the minimum components of termination pay and, where applicable, severance pay as mandated by the Ontario *Employment Standards Act, 2000*. It is also pay in lieu of reasonable notice as assessed by a judge at common law.

tort. A civil wrong, as contrasted with a criminal wrong, for which the wrongdoer is said to owe a legal duty to the injured party for conduct that falls below acceptable standards and for which the injured party can prove loss resulting from the wrongdoer's conduct.

vicarious liability. In the employment context, employer liability for the conduct of an employee causing loss to third parties. Liability is imposed on the employer as if the employer had caused the losses.

workplace administrative tribunal. Tribunals are not courts. Workplace administrative tribunals are specialized dispute adjudication forums created by the provincial government to decide blame and liability for the violation of certain provincial laws dealing with employment issues or the violation of a collective agreement's terms.

Unlike the judges in courts, tribunal appointees are not necessarily trained lawyers, and tribunals are not "courts of record," meaning that there are no transcripts of proceedings unless one of the parties before the tribunal chooses to engage a shorthand reporter, which can be done only with the tribunal's permission. The decisions of Ontario workplace administrative tribunals can be overturned (appealed) only by making application for judicial review to the Divisional Court.

The following are the primary private sector workplace administrative tribunals in Ontario:

- Human Rights Tribunal of Ontario (HRTO)
- Ontario Labour Relations Board (OLRB)
- Pay Equity Hearings Tribunal
- Workplace Safety and Insurance Appeals Tribunal

An arbitrator appointed under the provisions of a collective agreement is also a workplace administrative tribunal. In addition to the above list, there are specialized workplace administrative tribunals that deal with specific public sector employment issues, for example, the Grievance Settlement Board for Ontario, which adjudicates the grievances of Crown employees in the Ontario public service.

wrongful dismissal lawsuit. Legal claim advanced against an employer by a dismissed employee who is seeking damages for loss of employment.

Index

About the Author

Paul Wearing advises company presidents, CEOs, and HR managers on all aspects of employment and labour law to effectively manage the workplace. His law practice includes strategic labour and employment advice, training, and representation of private and public sector employers before the courts, the Ontario Labour Relations Board, the Canada Industrial Relations Board, and the Human Rights Tribunal of Ontario. Paul was called to the Ontario bar in 1978 and was counsel to the Association of Local Public Health Agencies before the Walkerton Commission of Inquiry.

His royalties from the sale of this book are donated to the Pediatric Cancer Research Foundation.

Printed and bound by CPI Group (UK) Ltd, Croydon, CR0 4YY

30/06/2026

14910916-0005